Let's Make Music!

Multicultural Songs And Activities

by Jessica Baron Turner and Ronny Susan Schiff

An Interactive Musical Trip Around The World

- Sing and play songs from around the world

- Create instruments from 10 different countries using recycled materials

Edited by Ronny Susan Schiff
Photographs by Heather Harris

HAL•LEONARD™

Acknowledgements

To all those who assisted in the creation of this book...
Rick Turner, the Baron Family, Mrs. E.H. Turner, Martin & Jessica Simpson, the Schenkkan family, John Nagy, Debbie Anderson & George Madaraz, Matt Cartsonis, Marty McKenzie, the Cooder family, M.B. Gordy, Paul Arnoldi, Paula & Paul Reiser, the staff, teachers and children at Lyric Preschool, Temple Isaiah Preschool, Old Town School of Folk Music, Telluride Bluegrass Academy, The Children's Music Network, David Lusterman, Jeffrey Pepper Rogers and the folks at Acoustic Guitar Magazine, Camille Ameen, Ira Ingber, Irwin Coster, Carolyn Mosoff, Maureen Woods, Connie Ambrosch, and the musicians, friends and their families who gave of their talents, good ideas and enthusiasm. Special thanks to Pete Seeger for a lifetime of inspiration. And to Melinda Wyant, Emily Crocker, John Higgins, and Herman Knoll at Hal Leonard for extending this opportunity. *Thank you.*

Children's hands provided by: Daniele Amos, Sydney Brown, André de Sant'anna

Special thanks to Pat Van Alyea and the Staff at "The Book Bay," Whitefish Bay, Wisconsin for compiling children's literature lists.

The activities set forth in this book should be conducted under the supervision of an adult. The authors and publisher specifically disclaim any liability, loss or risk, personal or otherwise, which is incurred as a consequence, directly or indirectly, of the use and application of any of the activities set forth herein.

Warning: Patent pending for book cover and audio packaging.

The purchase of this book entitles the buyer to duplicate the reproducible lyric pages only for use in the buyer's classroom. Any other use requires prior written permission of the publisher. Reproduction of these materials for an entire school or school system is strictly prohibited.

 Songs Copyright © 1994, 1995 Knobby Knees Music

For your convenience, this book is printed with a double cover. You may either store the recording in the compartment or tear off the outer cover and still have a book that is intact.

Library of Congress Cataloguing-in-Publication Data

Turner, Jessica Baron.
     Let's make music! : multicultural songs and activities : create your own instruments from around the world, sing and play a song for each instrument with the accompanying recording : by Jessica Baron Turner & Ronny Susan Schiff : edited by Ronny Susan Schiff.
        p.   cm.
       1. Musical instruments—Construction—Juvenile literature.
   2. Children's songs. 3. Games with music. I. Schiff, Ronny S.
   II. Title.
ML460.T89 1994
784—dc20

94-29340
CIP
MN AC

Book/Cassette Package: ISBN 0-7935-4056-9
Book/CD Package: ISBN 0-7935-4507-7

HAL•LEONARD™
CORPORATION
7777 W. BLUEMOUND RD. P.O.BOX 13819 MILWAUKEE, WI 53213

Contents

Biographies

Jessica Baron Turner, holds an M.A. in Marriage, Family and Child Counseling and is a Child Development specialist with an emphasis in music education, learning styles and strategies. She coordinates and teaches middle school programs in Human Development and Community Service at Crossroads School, Santa Monica, California. A vocalist, guitarist and songwriter since age 16, she has been teaching music to children since 1981. In the past she has served as Arts/Crafts/Music/Activities Family Area coordinator for the Telluride Bluegrass Festival. She lives with her husband, guitar maker Rick Turner, and their two cats in Topanga Canyon, California.

Ronny Susan Schiff, B.A., is an Early Childhood Music Specialist, Editor/Author of Early Childhood Song & Activity Books, Guest Lecturer for Los Angeles City School System Career Planning Seminars in Music & Graphics, and instructor for Los Angeles Pierce College Extension and the University Of California, Los Angeles Extension Music Division. She has edited or co-written over two thousand music collections and music methods, in print and CD ROM. She lives in a western ranch house in Van Nuys, California.

Introduction

As you read the pages that follow, a world of creative activities will come to life at your children's fingertips. Each activity has been carefully designed for the education and enjoyment of young children and those who guide them. *Let's Make Music!* brings arts, crafts, movement, games, world culture and music together with recycling! Have fun while you help care for our planet.

In this book, you'll find easy-to-follow instructions for making and playing percussion instruments from around the world. The photographs, patterns, clear language, and music and rhythm lines will help you and your children be successful immediately. Your musical instruments will look and sound wonderful. They also make exciting gifts.

When an instrument is constructed, join us and play along with the *Let's Make Music!* recording. You can travel to ten countries, singing new lyrics to each country's traditional melodies. Each set of lyric gives children insight into the culture, geography or animal life of the various countries. The recording features musical instruments and arrangements native to each culture, with easy-to-hear percussion parts to make playing along easy and fun.

Use *Let's Make Music!* in whatever sequence works best for you. Whether you take the musical journey around the world and build as you go, or select projects out of sequence, we know you will have a delightful adventure. Please let us know how things are coming along. And if you can, keep the glue off the doorknobs.

—*Jessica Baron Turner & Ronny Susan Schiff*

How To Prepare

To begin making each instrument, simply refer to the "Materials" lists to decide which materials to collect. Then gather them along with the few necessary household items, and you're set in but a short time (see *Recycled Materials And Resource Guide*, page 65, for suggested places to find materials).

"Time Needed" recommendations are computed by 20 minute to half hour time periods.

The "Craft Skills" lists alert you to specific skills that children will be employing in the activity.

The "Concepts" lists refer to the various concepts, vocabulary and movement skills that children may be learning while making these instruments.

The "Vocabulary" section refers to the new words introduced in the songs.

The "Helping Hand" symbols ☞ determine which steps work best with adult assistance.

For even more fun, read some of the books listed in the "Books To Read" section and organize the special activities that incorporate the use of the instrument in a story, game or movement.

How To Play Along With The Recording

Each song on the recording has a percussion introduction along with which a child can play his or her instrument to a *steady beat*. The *steady beat* and special rhythms for the songs are indicated on the music with diagonal lines (/).

Refer back to the book and the photographs of how to hold each instrument and the instructions on how to play it. During the introduction, guide children in holding the instrument and showing them how to play along with each steady beat. Encourage them to learn the lyrics and sing along.

If a child shows an ability for playing more complex or syncopated rhythms, or understands the concept of playing on every other beat, such as 1 and 3, let 'em go! They'll really be making music!

Make Maracas!

From Mexico

In Mexico, the round, hollow parts of rhythm instruments are traditionally made from wood or coconut shells! These are filled with small pebbles, kernels of uncooked corn, or seeds. Next, the shells are fitted with wooden handles, which are glued into place. Finally, the maracas are decorated with paint and shellac.

Your maracas are easier to make. They are also prettier to watch, since you can see their contents bounce around as you play them. You are helping out the environment too, because you'll be recycling two plastic bottles for each pair of maracas that you make.

Time Needed: Two class periods—one to prepare filler, one for construction.

CRAFT SKILLS

- applying tape or contact paper
- cutting
- pouring solids
- sorting by appearances
- twisting bottle tops
- wrapping

CONCEPTS

up, down, left, right, shake, toward, away

VOCABULARY

blanco—white
chiles —a very hot small pepper
olé—a shout of approval
rojo—red
tortilla—a round, flat Mexican bread
verde—green

MATERIALS NEEDED

- clear cylindrical plastic bottles with long necks
- beans
- uncooked popcorn
- uncooked rice
- scouring pad
- rubber "electrical" tape or bicycle grip tape
- piece of paper, 8 ½ inches x 11 inches
- scissors

Make Maracas

1. ☞ In three separate dishes, pour rice, beans and kernels of uncooked popcorn. If you want to color these items, use the food color/denatured alcohol technique (see page 51) ahead of time. You may also want to use pebbles. (*Note:* These cannot be colored using food coloring.)

2. ☞ Wash your plastic bottle. Soak off the label. Use the scouring pad to scrub off any stubborn paper or glue residue.

3. Take the cap off the bottle.

4. ☞ Make a paper funnel by rolling up a piece of paper into an ice cream cone shape. Put the narrow end into the mouth of the bottle and make the end in the air wider by pulling gently at the sides of the paper. *(See Figure 1.)*

Figure 1

5. Take a handful of popcorn, rice or beans and drop them into the top of your paper funnel. Now shake the bottle gently and listen to the sound. *(See Figure 2.)*

6. If you want a louder maraca or a different sound, add another kind of filler or some more of the same.

7. When you are happy with the sound of your maraca, put the cap back on your bottle.

8. ☞ Wrap the tape around the top and neck of your bottles. This will seal the maraca and provide an easy place on which to hold. You can use more than one color of tape to decorate the maraca handles.

Figure 2

Play Maracas

1. To play a maraca, place the handle of the instrument across the palm of your hand. Wrap your fingers securely around the handle. Close your hand by resting a thumb on the handle, above the fingers. Now you are ready to shake the maracas. *(See Figure 3)*

2. To shake your maracas, bend your arms up at the elbows. Raise them toward your face. Then shake them away from you very quickly. Stop when the maracas are level with your chest. You should hear the maracas when your arms stop moving. Repeat these *toward* and *away* motions with a steady beat—*1,2,3, 1,2,3. (See Figure 4)*

3. Often, maracas are played one at a time. First shake one, then shake the other. Practice shaking your maracas in a pattern now:

   Left, right, left, right,

   Together, together, together, together

   Repeat this from the beginning.

4. In the song, "These Are The Colors I Know," the steady beat comes in groups of three—*1,2,3.* This is a common rhythmic pattern in Mexican music. Here is a maraca pattern to practice before you play along with the song:

   Left, right, left; together, together, together

   Right, left, right; together, together, together

Figure 3

Figure 4

Read A Book

1. All of You Was Singing (Gr. 3-6)
by Richard Lewis (Atheneum)
The retelling of this Aztec myth concerns the creation of Earth and the beginning of music.

2. The Bravest Flute: A Story of Courage in the Mayan Tradition (Pre K-3)
by Ann Grifalconi (Little, Brown, and Company)
A brave boy leads a parade of farmers across the mountains to the big town for the annual New Year's celebration.

3. De Colores and Other Latin American Folk Songs for Children (Pre K-4)
selected, arranged and translated
by José-Luis Orozco (Dutton)
A collection of 27 songs, chants and rhymes that are loved by children all over Latin America.

4. Margaret and Margarita, Margarita and Margaret (Pre K-2)
by Lynn Reiser (Greenwillow)
Bilingual English and Spanish text. Two preschoolers meet in the park and enjoy the day though they speak two languages.

5. Nine Days To Christmas (Pre K-3)
by Marie Hall Ets and Aurora Labastida (Viking)
A girl accompanies her mother to the market to choose a piñata.

Rainbow Chaser
A Tag Game with Maracas

This game gives children a chance to play maracas and learn to say their colors in Spanish. It can be played by three or more people.

1. Choose one child to be the first *Rainbow Chaser*. This child stands in the center of the play area and holds the maracas ready to play.

2. Then choose one child to be the *Olla* de Oro* (Pot of Gold). The Olla stands five paces away from the Rainbow Chaser.

3. Each of the other children chooses to "be" one color for his or her role in this round of the game. Two or more children may share the name of a single color. The leader may assist the children in saying the names of their colors in Spanish.

> white—*blanco*
> red—*rojo*
> pink—*clavel*
> orange—*naranja*
> yellow—*amarillo*
> green—*verde*
> blue—*azul*
> brown—*moreno*
> black—*negro*

4. The game begins with the "colors" gathered around the Rainbow Chaser and the Olla de Oro. The Olla de Oro walks five paces to the Rainbow Chaser and clearly announces the name of a color in Spanish.

5. The Rainbow Chaser shakes the maracas ten times, giving the named "color" player(s) a chance to run away.

6. Now a game of tag begins between the named "color" player(s) and the Rainbow Chaser. The object of the game is for the Rainbow Chaser to tag the named "color" player(s) on the shoulder.

7. When the named "color" player is caught, he or she becomes the new Rainbow Chaser. The Rainbow Chaser becomes the new Olla de Oro and children select new colors to play for the next round.

*In Spanish the double "L" is pronounced like a "Y," therefore "Olla" is pronounced "Oya."

These Are The Colors I Know

(Based on the music of "Chiapanecas")

Music Adaptation and New Lyric by
Jessica Baron Turner

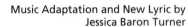

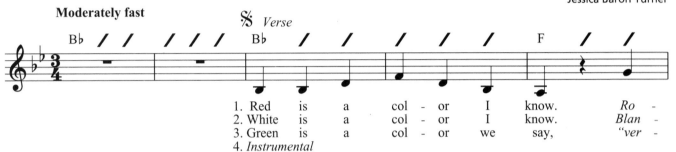

Moderately fast

1. Red is a col - or I know. *Ro -*
2. White is a col - or I know. *Blan -*
3. Green is a col - or we say, *"ver -*
4. *Instrumental*

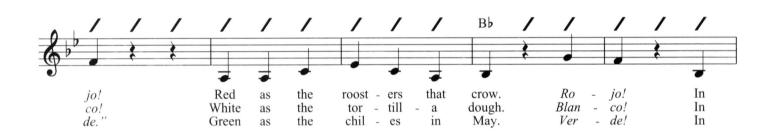

jo! Red as the roost - ers that crow. *Ro - jo!* In
co! White as the tor - till - a dough. *Blan - co!* In
de." Green as the chil - es in May. *Ver - de!* In

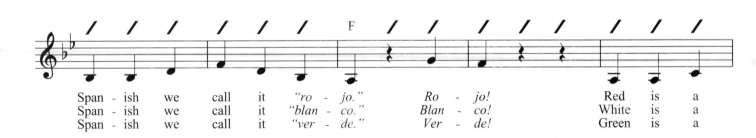

Span - ish we call it *"ro - jo."* *Ro - jo!* Red is a
Span - ish we call it *"blan - co."* *Blan - co!* White is a
Span - ish we call it *"ver - de."* *Ver - de!* Green is a

Chorus (no repeat first time)

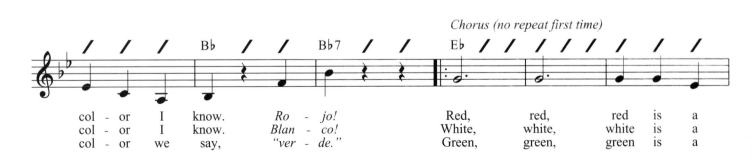

col - or I know. *Ro - jo!* Red, red, red is a
col - or I know. *Blan - co!* White, white, white is a
col - or we say, *"ver - de."* Green, green, green is a

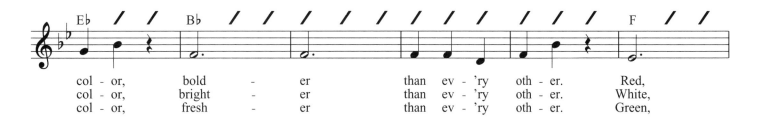

col - or, bold - er than ev - 'ry oth - er. Red,
col - or, bright - er than ev - 'ry oth - er. White,
col - or, fresh - er than ev - 'ry oth - er. Green,

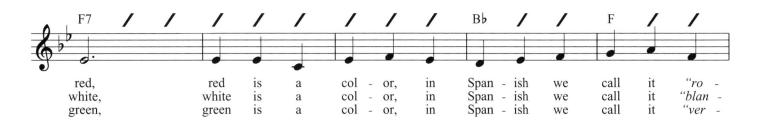

red, red is a col - or, in Span - ish we call it *"ro -*
white, white is a col - or, in Span - ish we call it *"blan -*
green, green is a col - or, in Span - ish we call it *"ver -*

**Repeat as needed,
then D.S.**

CODA

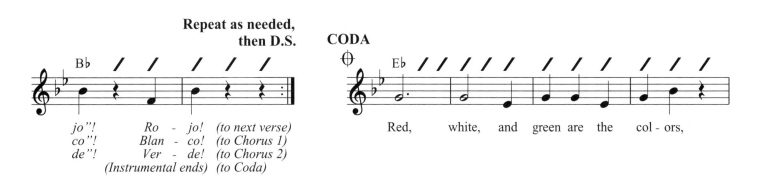

jo"! Ro - jo! (to next verse)
co"! Blan - co! (to Chorus 1)
de"! Ver - de! (to Chorus 2)
(Instrumental ends) (to Coda)

Red, white, and green are the col - ors,

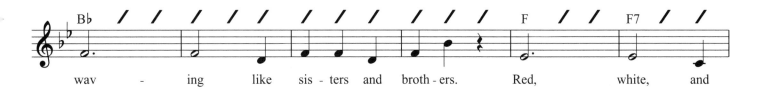

wav - ing like sis - ters and broth - ers. Red, white, and

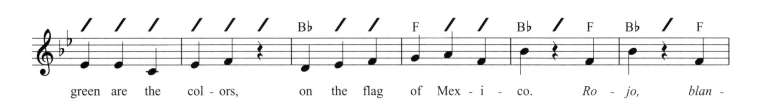

green are the col - ors, on the flag of Mex - i - co. *Ro - jo, blan -*

co, ver - de, o - lé! _____

Make A Rainstick!

From Chile

In Chile, this instrument is made from the skeleton of a cactus, filled with cactus spines. The sound it makes is like falling raindrops. Native Chilean people* have traditionally used this stick in religious ceremonies as a way of calling for rains to come.

Today, rainsticks are made many different ways. They always have a long round tube for a shell and are filled with tiny metal pellets or small, hard objects inside. Something inside the tube must act as a baffle, slowing the pellets down so they fall gradually instead of all at once. In Chile, cactus spines are pulled out, turned around and pushed into the tube to slow the pellets down. However, sharp objects are dangerous, so we suggest a safe method that uses heavy paper or thin cardboard instead.

*Diaguita Indians

Time Needed: Two class periods—one class period to color the rice, measure and cut the baffles. One class period to tape the baffles together, drop them into the tube, add rice, and seal and decorate the rainstick.

CRAFT SKILLS

- tracing
- cutting
- folding
- taping
- wrapping or paper tearing
- gluing
- pouring

CONCEPTS

on top of, triangle, through, upside down, continuous motion

VOCABULARY

canta—sing
cu, cu, ru—the sound a dove makes
pajarito—little bird

MATERIALS NEEDED

- one clear, plastic postal tube
  - or one cardboard tube from inside a large roll of wrapping paper
- two large pieces of heavy paper or tag board (oak tag, cereal box cardboard, dry cleaning collar cardboard, note pad backing, etc.)
- scissors
- filler such as uncooked popcorn, sand, bird seed, or rice
- two plastic lids from recyclable containers (optional)
- masking or clear tape
- duct tape
- yarn
- glue

Make A Rainstick

1 ☞ First you will make the triangle shapes that serve as baffles for your rainstick. Using a ruler, measure the diameter of the opening of your tube. Multiply this number by 3, then subtract ½ an inch. The answer to this math problem tells you how long each strip of paper must be. Encourage children to watch! This is a demonstration of mathematics in action.

Example: If the diameter of your tube is 2 inches, each strip of paper must be 5 ½ inches long. *(See Figure 1.)*

2 ☞ Using scissors or a paper cutter, prepare 20 strips of paper or cardboard 1 ½ inches wide and as long as your final calculation from step number one. Children can help with this process if you give them a line along which to cut. If your rainstick tube is clear, you may want to have the children decorate the strips of paper now before moving on to step three.

3 ☞ Demonstrate how to fold each strip of paper into thirds. Hold one end of the strip and bend it over the middle of the strip. Push it down and make a crease. Now take the other end and bend it over the first one. *(See Figure 2.)*

4 ☞ Tape the two ends together to make a triangle. Children will enjoy helping with the bending, creasing, and taping. *(See Figure 3.)*

5 Put a bottom on the tube. You can easily make one out of the lid from a plastic container by tracing the circumference of the tube onto the plastic lid, then cutting it out. Finally, tape the bottom into place using strong duct tape.

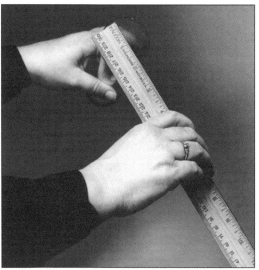

Figure 1

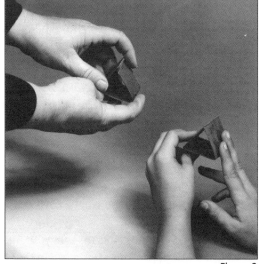

Figure 2

Figure 3

6 Now you are ready to add the triangle baffles. Drop the finished triangles one at a time into the tube. Their three points should almost touch the inside edges of the tube. *(See Figure 4.)*

7 Next, take a handful of filler and drop it into the tube. Listen to the filler as it falls against the baffles. Continue to add more filler until you are pleased with the rain sound effect.

8 ☞ Now seal the rainstick with a top. If you don't have one, make one just like you made for the bottom of the tube.

9 Your rainstick is ready to be decorated. You can do this many different ways, but we suggest covering it with yarn, unless your rainstick is clear. Then it's fun to watch the filler bounce off of the baffles as it falls.

10 To wrap your rainstick in yarn, begin by taping one end of the yarn to the outside of the tube, one inch from the bottom. *(See Figure 5.)*

11 ☞ Now begin wrapping the yarn around the stick from the bottom, upwards. When the stick is wrapped, your tape will be covered!

12 ☞ To vary the colors of yarn, you can change from one color to another by tying the old and new ends together in a small, tight knot. Then just keep wrapping until the whole stick is covered.

13 ☞ Complete the wrapping by tucking the loose end underneath the already wound yarn. Brush it with glue to keep it from unraveling later! When the glue is dry, you are ready to play. *(See Figure 6.)*

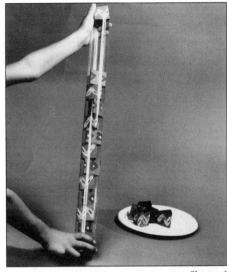

Figure 4

Figure 5

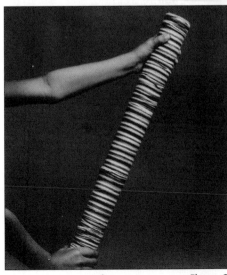

Figure 6

Play The Rainstick

- To play the rainstick, grasp it at each end. If it's very long, hold it toward the center using both hands. Keep your hands about a foot apart. Either way, hold the rainstick at a diagonal angle and gently turn it from end to end, like a baton. *(See Figure 7.)*

- As long as you turn the rainstick while the filler is still falling, the rain sound will keep going. If you wait until all the filler has landed at the bottom of the rainstick before you turn it, there will be a pause in the sound.

- If you wish to play the rainstick in a non-traditional way, hold it parallel to the ground, several inches away from your body. Shake it toward and away from you like a maraca to play it rhythmically.

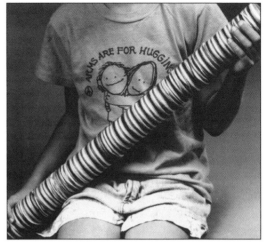

Figure 7

Read A Book

1. ***Arroz Con Leche: Popular Songs and Rhymes for Latin America* (Pre K-2)**
   by Lulu Delacre (Scholastic)
   Games, music, poetry, and rhymes from Latin America.

2. ***At Home In The Rainforest* (Gr. 2-4)**
   by Diana Willow (Charles Bridge)
   Each page and one-half spread depicts a moment in the Amazon rain forest.
   Brief descriptions of native plants and animals.

3. ***The Great Kapok Tree: A Tale of the Amazon Rain Forest* (Pre K-3)**
   by Lynne Cherry (Harcourt Brace)
   This is a story about the incredible beauty of the rain forest and the creatures that inhabit it.

4. ***Junglewalk* (Pre K-2)**
   by Nancy Tafuri (Greenwillow)
   A wordless journey through the rain forest.

5. ***Moon Rope* (K-2)**
   by Louis Ehlert (Harcourt Brace Jovanovich)
   A Peruvian folk tale about a fox that wants to go to the moon.

6. ***Tortillittas Para Mama and Other Nursery Rhymes: Spanish and English* (Pre K-2)**
   by Barbara Cooney (Holt)
   13 well-known Latino nursery rhymes.

Rain or Shine

A Movement Game With The Rainstick

Similar to the well-known game *Red Light, Green Light,* this game will help children develop listening skills in addition to a quick auditory-motor response. It also gives children practice playing the rainstick without causing a break in the "raining" sound.

This game requires an open space such as a playground, field, a room without furniture in the middle, or a wide corridor. You will need to create two playing stations: One is simply a place in which the leader will always stand. The other is a line set fifteen feet or more behind the leader. If you are working on linoleum, tile, or concrete surfaces, you can make this line with masking tape, on grass with a piece of rope or brightly colored yarn.

1. The leader takes a rainstick to the front of the playing area. The rest of the group stands behind the line. The leader turns her or his back to the group and calls out the word "RAIN!"

2. The leader now plays the rainstick continuously, turning it over and over again. As he or she does this, the rest of players try to sneak up quietly on the leader.

3. Whenever the leader chooses, he or she stops playing the rainstick and turns around, shouting the word "SUNSHINE!" At the moment the players hear the rainstick stop, they attempt to freeze in place.

4. The leader tries to catch any players who are still moving. Anyone who is caught goes back behind the starting line again and starts his or her journey to the leader all over.

5. The first player to reach the front of the playing area must touch the leader on the shoulder. That player may become the new leader or may choose someone else for the job. The new leader begins the game anew by calling out the word "RAIN!" and starts playing the rainstick continuously.

Canta, Canta Pretty Dove (Sing, Sing Pretty Dove)

(Based on the music of "Canta, Canta Pajarito")

Music Adaptation and New Lyric by
Jessica Baron Turner

Moderately

dove.   Can - ta, can-ta pa - ja - ri - to,   in the spring you sing a song of love.

Can - ta, can-ta, pa - ja - ri - to;   { can - ta, can-ta, pret-ty dove.   Can - ta, can-ta, pa - ja -
can - ta, can-ta, cu, cu, ru.   Can - ta, can-ta, pa - ja -

ri - to,   feel the rain - drops fall-ing from a - bove.
ri - to,   how the show - ers help the flow-ers   bloom.   Can - ta, can-ta, pa - ja -

ri - to;   can - ta, can-ta, pret-ty dove.   Can - ta, can-ta, pa - ja - ri - to,   in the

spring you sing a song of love.   Can - ta, can-ta, pa - ja - ri - to;   can - ta, can-ta, as you

fly.   Can - ta, can-ta, pa - ja - ri - to,   see the rain - bow col-or-ing the sky.

rit.

Make Clappers!

From Australia

Clappers, also known as *boomerang clapsticks,* come from the Aboriginal (native) people of Australia. Ours look a lot like boomerangs, but are used only to make rhythmic music. Clappers are held one in each hand, grasped in the middle or toward the bottom, and clapped together.

Time Needed: Two class periods—one for construction, one for decoration.

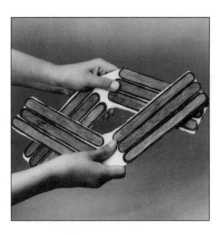

CRAFT SKILLS
- tracing
- cutting
- gluing
- painting.

CONCEPTS
on top of, middle, bottom, together, around

VOCABULARY
boomerang —a flat, V-shaped piece of wood that when thrown can be made to return to the thrower
bush—in Australia, the countryside
eucalyptus—a tall Australian tree; cough drops are made from its sap
haw—the laughing sound that a kookaburra makes
joey—a baby kangaroo
kangaroo—an Australian animal with short front legs and long back legs, who jumps instead of walking, and keeps its baby in a pouch
koala bear—an Australian animal that looks like a little bear and lives in trees
kookaburra—a noisy Australian bird

MATERIALS NEEDED

- two 6 inch by 2 inch strips of heavy cardboard
- 24 tongue depressors or ice cream sticks
- white glue
- one pencil
- scissors
- marking pen

Make Clappers

1. ☞ Trace or cut out the pattern for clappers from the *Appendix*.

2. Place the pattern on top of your cardboard and trace it. Now do this again on a second piece of cardboard. *(See Figure 1.)*

3. Cut along the outer line you traced. This piece of cardboard will be the inside of your clappers.

4. Squeeze a generous amount of glue onto one side of each clapper. Use a paint brush to spread the glue evenly across the entire surface.

5. Pick up a tongue depressor and press it down onto the glue-covered cardboard at one end of the clapper. Put another one next to it, and add a third, just as the picture illustrates. *(See Figure 2.)*

6. Now do the same thing again at the bottom end of the clapper, using three tongue depressors. Let these one-sided clappers dry overnight.

7. When the first sides of the clappers are dry, repeat steps four, five, and six to their other sides. Both sides of the clappers should be covered with wood so you can use them in every direction and combination.

8. When the clappers are dry, decorate the wood by drawing on it with markers. Now you are ready to play. *(See Figure 3.)*

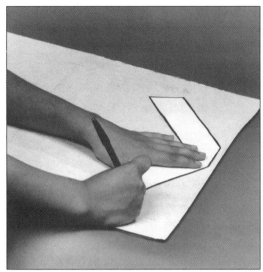

Figure 1

Figure 2

Figure 3

Play The Clappers

- Place the clappers so that their centers point away from each other, like two arrows going in opposite directions

- Grasp a clapper in each hand at its bend in the middle. Now hold the clappers parallel to the ground.

- Place your thumbs flatly on each clapper top, and press the rest of your fingertips together against the bottom side of each clapper. *(See Figure 4.)*

- Hit the tops of the clappers together lightly.

- Hit the bottom of the clappers together lightly.

- Clap them together to a rhythm!

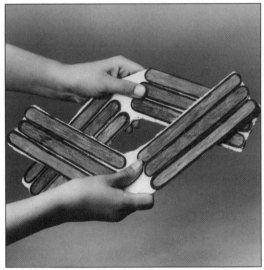

Figure 4

Read A Book

1. Crocodile Snaps! Kangaroo Jumps **(Pre K)**
by Daniel Lehan (Orchard)
A crocodile chases a person and eats his or her boots with a snap of its jaws; the book can be turned upside-down to depict the story of the stubborn kangaroo that finally leaps.

2. Dreamtime **(Pre K-2)**
by Oodgeroo (Lothrop, Lee and Shepard)
This book shares read-aloud stories about the author's childhood on an island off the Queensland coast and stories of Aboriginal folklore. An unusual and delightful collection.

3. Koala Lou **(Pre K-3)**
by Mem Fox (Harcourt Brace)
A young koala, longing to hear her mother speak lovingly to her, as she did before other children came along, plans to win her distracted parents' attention.

4. One Wooly Wombat **(Pre K-2)**
by Rod Trinca and Kerry Argent (Kane-Miller Books)
A counting book that teaches the numbers 1-14 as well as presenting delightful rhymes about Australian animal life.

One, Two, Kangaroo
A Counting Game for the Clappers

This game gives children the opportunity to count from one to eight with their clappers while they recite a rhyme with an Australian theme. It can be considered a "math readiness" activity and it assists children with the development of spoken language, rhythm, and better listening skills. By practicing clapping beats in sequences, and with repetition, they can learn the rhyme. The game can be played by two or more people. Here is the rhyme with notation showing long and short beats:

"One, Two, Kangaroo" — The Rhyme

-   - - - - -   -

One, koala having fun. (*clap*)

—   —   -   - -

One, two, kangaroo.
(*clap clap*)

-   -   —   -   -   -

One, two, three, wallaby.
(*clap clap clap*)

—   —   —   —

One, two, three, four,

-   - - - -   -

kookaburra by my door.
(*clap clap clap clap*)

—   —   -   -   —

One, two, three, four, five,

-   - - -   - --

all of nature is alive.
(*clap clap clap clap clap*)

-   -   -   -   -   -   —

One, two, three, four, five and six,

-   - - - -   -   —

platypuses playing tricks.
(*clap clap clap clap clap clap*)

-   -   -   -   -   -   - -

One, two, three, four, five, six, seven,

-   -   -   -   -   -   -

Southern Lights are in the heavens.
(*clap clap clap clap clap clap clap*)

-   -   -   -   -   -   -   -

One, two, three, four, five, six, seven, eight,

- - - - - -   —

I call all my buddies "mate."
(*clap clap clap clap clap clap clap clap*)

The Game

1. Ask players to form a circle. The group can play standing up or sitting down. Each player must have his or her own pair of clappers.

2. Until children have learned to recite the rhyme "One, Two, Kangaroo," an adult should be the leader. Once they know the rhyme, children can become leaders, as well.

3. The leader makes sure that all the players are holding their clappers correctly and are ready to play. Then she begins the rhyme by reciting, *"One koala having fun,"* then claps her clappers just once at the end of the line. The players pass this single beat around the circle, one at a time, as each player, in order, claps his or her clappers together once.

   Note: If anyone claps their clappers more than once, the whole recitation and playing begins over again! This makes for lots of laughter.

4. Now the leader recites, *"One two kangaroo"* and claps her clappers twice. The players pass these two beats around the circle, one at a time, as each player claps his or her clappers together twice.

   Challenge the players to create a beautiful, unbroken rhythm as they pass the beats around the circle. The rule about starting over if someone misses a beat applies throughout the game.

5. The leader chooses the highest number her circle should attempt to play, based on the group's ability to succeed. If a group reaches *"One, two, three, four, kookaburra by my door,"* but is struggling with clapping for five counts on the next round, the game should end there. As children develop their counting skills, the final number will be a larger one.

   Challenge: If children are successful counting and clapping to eight, write new lines to fit the next numbers in your sequence. You may wish to use this as an opportunity for everyone to learn more about Australia.

We'll Go A-Walking About In The Bush
(Based on the music of "Craigielea")

Music Adaptation and New Lyric by
Jessica Baron Turner

Make A Pien Chung!

From China

In China, the pien chung is made by hanging brass bells in a row. Each bell dangles at the end of a small ring, and the rings are attached to a large, standing frame. Our version of the pien chung is easier to make. You can use recyclable or everyday items from around your home and neighborhood.

Time Needed: One class period (once you've collected the materials).

CRAFT SKILLS

- tying knots
- twisting pipe cleaners
- threading

CONCEPTS

striking, balancing, identifying high and low sounds

VOCABULARY

bamboo—a type of grass that looks like hollow, hard sticks
chan mali chew—nonsense words like "ee-i-ee-i-o"
crane—a bird with a very long neck that likes to wade in the water
koi—a fish found in China and Japan that looks like a big goldfish
panda—a very large black and white Chinese bear

MATERIALS NEEDED

- one long, thick cardboard tube from a roll of wrapping paper
- two 8-10 inch pieces of string
  - or one dowel rod *and* two 8"-10" pieces of string
  - or one yard of clothes line
- two stable chairs of the same height
- two metal spoons
- six or more plastic wire trash bag ties or pipe cleaners
- six or more metallic or stone items that can be suspended from trash bag ties or pipe cleaners, such as…
  - old keys all strung together
  - an old vegetable strainer or steamer
  - a spatula
  - a pot or pan lid
  - nuts, bolts or washers
  - a bandage box
  - cans with dull edges (you can dull any edge by covering it with duct tape)

Make A Pien Chung

1. ☞ Set up your crosspiece. If you are using clothesline, tie both ends to something stable and within a child's reach.
   If you are using a dowel or cardboard tube, tie the ends to the tops of the backs of two chairs. Make sure your crosspiece is secure. *(See Figure 1.)*

2. ☞ Gather your household or neighborhood items. Using a tablespoon, tap the items you are considering for your pien chung. Choose the sounds you like, but exercise discretion regarding safety. Sharp or pointy items should not be used.

3. ☞ Run a wire tie or pipe cleaner around a handle or protuberance or through a hole on the first item you wish to hang. Leave two inches of the tie free like a tail for closing the loop in Step 4. *(See Figure 2.)*

4. ☞ Now run the wire tie or pipe cleaner up and over the top of your crosspiece, then bring it back down again. Close the loop by twisting the end securely around the "tail" five times. Now your item should be hanging freely from the crosspiece. *(See Figure 3.)*

5. ☞ Before hanging your next item, listen to the sound of the one you just hung. Do you want the next item to sound higher or lower in pitch than the first? What about the third, fourth and so on? You can put your pien chung items in order according to size, shape, color or sound. (See Figure 4.)

Figure 1

Figure 2

Figure 3

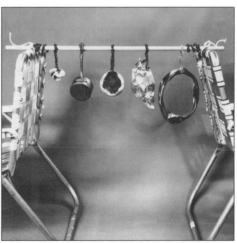

Figure 4

Play The Pien Chung

- Hold a metal spoon by the handle in each hand. Use the round part of the spoon to hit the pien chung. *(See Figure 5.)*

- Play each sound on the pien chung by striking each item with the spoon. Now play two items at the same time. Find sounds that you like. Does anything you play remind you of sounds you hear every day?

- When playing the pien chung with music, strike the hanging items along with the steady beat or beat a rhythm on them using one or both hands.

Figure 5

Read A Book

1. At The Beach (Ages 3-6)
by Huy Voun Lee (Holt)
A summer day at the beach is portrayed and introduces children to one of the oldest picture languages in the world, Chinese.

2. Chinese Mother Goose Rhymes (Pre K-3)
selected and edited by Robert Wyndham (Philomel)
An enchanting collection of poems, rhymes, and songs from the Chinese oral tradition.

3. Dumpling Soup (Pre K-4)
by Jama Kim Rattigan (Little Brown)
Marisa makes dumplings on New Years Eve for her family which is of Korean, Japanese, Chinese, Hawaiian, and white ancestry. Story takes place in Hawaii.

4. Emma's Dragon Hunt (Pre K-4)
by Catherine Stock (Lothrop)
Emma's grandfather arrives from China. He introduces her to dragon lore that is shown as storms, earthquakes, and other natural phenomena.

5. Lon Po Po – A Red Riding Hood Tale From China (Ages 4-8)
retold by Ed Young (Philomel Books)
This Chinese tale comes from the ancient oral tradition and is thought to be over one thousand years old. A Caldecott winner.

6. Rabbit Mooncakes
by Hoong Yee Lee Krakauer (Little, Brown, and Co.)
A young girl dreads her family's Harvest Moon festivities because she will be asked to play the piano. Text includes Chinese words.

7. The Rainbow People (Gr. 4-8)
Illustrated by David Wiesner (Harper Collins)
Collection of Chinese-American folk tales that reinforce Chinese traditions.

8. Tikki Tikki Tembo (Gr. 2-4)
by Arlene Masel (Holt)
The folktale of how the Chinese came to give their children short names.

A Closet Full Of Noise
A Rhythm Activity for the Pien Chung

In China, the melody or rhythm may often follow the story line of a song. Recite this rhyme with the children as they hit the pien chung to the steady beat. Pause between each of the lines in the second stanza, so that children play the pien chung for three beats (////) before the next line begins.

Johnny has a closet

filled with toys.

When he opens up the door,

out comes noise.

Down come the markers, ///

down come the skates, ///

down come the marbles, ///

and the plastic plates. ///

Jenny has a closet

filled with toys.

When she opens up the door,

out comes noise.

Down come the markers, ///

down come the skates, ///

down come the marbles, ///

and the plastic plates. ///

After children learn the rhyme, replace the names in the rhyme with the names of children from your group.

Chan Mali Chew
(Based on the music of "Can Mali Can")

Music Adaptation and New Lyric by
Jessica Baron Turner and Paula Ravets

Additional Lyrics

4. I have a shiny fish,
   it is a koi.
   It gurgles like a girl,
   but it bubbles like a boy.
   We don't know what to name it,
   so we call it Billy Sue.
   Chan mali, chan mali,
   chan mali chew.
   Chorus

5. I have a furry panda,
   he kisses and he hugs.
   He looks a lot like Grandma,
   but he likes to play with bugs.
   He washes in the water
   and he brushes with bamboo.
   Chan mali, chan mali,
   chan mali chew.
   Chorus

Make A Wood Scraper!

From India

Wood scrapers can be found in different parts of the world. They all share the same basic design: a straight or curved wooden surface covered with a row of raised pieces of wood. The wood is laid out like railroad tracks. The sound of wood scraping is popular in some Indian music, as well as in Latin American and Caribbean music.

Music in India may follow a story and have a dreamy, soft feeling or a very exciting feeling that lasts a long time. Some music is only played at a certain time of the day.

Time Needed: Two class periods—one period for construction, one period for decoration.

CRAFT SKILLS

- balancing
- gluing
- making patterns

CONCEPTS

next to, on top of, straight, even spacing, away, toward

VOCABULARY

jingles—small bells like jingle bells
tabla—a drum

MATERIALS NEEDED

- one cardboard tube from a roll of paper towels
- ten tongue depressors or ice cream sticks
- white glue
- two small unopened cans (tuna fish, cat food, water chestnuts)
- markers or tempera paint
- paintbrush or cotton swab for glue

Make A Wood Scraper

1 ☞ Place newspaper on your table. Put all the supplies in front of you. *(See Figure 1.)*

2 ☞ Put the paper towel tube in front of you on the newspaper. Hold it in place by setting one can on each side of it. Keep the cans there until the wood scraper is dry.

3 Apply a lot of glue along the top of the tube to cover the area as wide as the top of the tube.

4 ☞ Take a tongue depressor and lay it in the glue at one end of the tube so that it crosses the tube like a "t." *(See Figure 2.)*

5 Now take another tongue depressor and place it a finger's width away from the first one. Do this again and again until the entire length of the tube is crossed with tongue depressors. Make the tube look like a train track. *(See Figure 3.)*

6 Let the glue dry for at least an hour or overnight.

7 ☞ When the wood scraper is totally dry, decorate it by drawing on it with markers or painting it with tempera. Apply a final coat of glue on the entire instrument for a sealed, shiny surface.

8 Select a tongue depressor or any other kind of stick to use as the scraper.

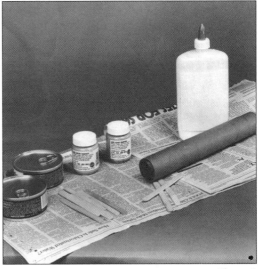

Figure 1

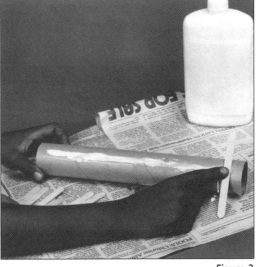

Figure 2

Figure 3

Play The Wood Scraper

- Hold the wood scraper upright in one hand and hold a stick in the palm of your other hand. *(See Figure 4.)*

- Run the end of your stick along the top of the scraper to make wonderful clicking sounds. If you play it very slowly, you can make it sound like a bull frog. Experiment playing it at different speeds or "tempos."

- Now try scraping the stick away from you a few times. Now scrape the stick toward you. Practice playing this pattern to the steady beat:
  away, toward, away, toward
  away, toward, away, toward

- Try this fancier pattern when you are ready. Begin by scraping away from yourself with one smooth, slow motion, then scrape toward yourself with two quick strokes.
  away, toward, toward; away, toward, toward
  slow quick quick; slow quick quick

- Feel free to experiment by making your own rhythmic patterns.

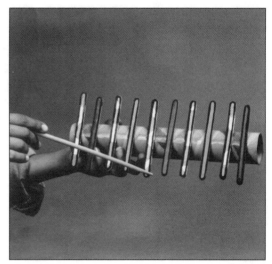

Figure 4

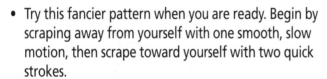

Read A Book

1. Anni's India Diary **(K-3)**
by Anni Axworth (Whispering)
Ten year old Anni gives an entertaining and informative impression of India through her diary entries about her family's trip.

2. Count Your Way Through India **(Gr. 1-4)**
by Jim Haskins (Carolrhoda Books)
A counting book that focuses on India and its culture.

3. Crocodile! Crocodile! Stories Told Around The World **(K-4)**
by Barbara Baumgartner (Dorling Kindersley)
An international collection of folk tales brings together six stories that can be read or brought to life by making stick puppets for acting out the stories.

4. The Jungle Book **(Pre K-4)**
By Rudyard Kipling
There are many publications available featuring this traditional adventure story from India.

Fast And Slow: The Conductor Game
A Movement Activity For The Wood Scraper

1. Invite children to walk around the room with their wood scrapers. Ask them to play the wood scraper every time they take another step. Ask them to walk quickly; then ask them to walk slowly. Finally, ask them to walk very slowly, as if in slow motion.

2. Now have the children come back and sit in a circle. Ask each child to show the others the speeds at which he or she walked by playing the wood scraper. If you have many children in the circle, ask each one to show "one way" or "one speed" they liked. You can help the children learn to name their walking tempos by pointing out which ones are *very slow, slow, moderate, quick,* and *very quick.*

3. Now invite a child to be the conductor. The conductor will clap to show what tempo she or he wants the children to play on their wood scrapers. If the conductor claps quickly, the children must follow. If the conductor slows down, so should the group.

4. Plan at least 20 minutes to play this game so that each child can have an opportunity to conduct. You'll probably be asked to play this game again and again. Young children love this experience of autonomy and being in charge.

We Dance With Love
(Based on the music of "Dancing With Gourds")

Music Adaptation and New Lyric by
Jessica Baron Turner

Slowly & dreamily

1. We play with scrap-ers and with sticks, here in In - di - a. Wood scrap-ers we are play-ing, hear us dance and sing.
2. We dance with jin-gles on our an - kles, here in In - di - a. Jin-gles up - on our an - kles, hear us dance and sing.
3. We drum up - on the pret - ty ta - blas, here in In - di - a. Drum-ming up - on the ta - blas, hear us dance and sing.
4. - 8. *See additional lyrics*

Wood scrap-ers we are play-ing, hear us dance and sing. _____
rit.

Additional Lyrics

4. *Instrumental*

5. We play for family and friends
   here in India.
   For all our family
   we love to dance and sing.

6. *Instrumental*

7. We dance with love inside our hearts,
   here in India.
   With love for everybody
   hear us dance and sing.

8. We play with scrapers and with sticks,
   here in India.
   Wood scrapers we are playing,
   hear us dance and sing.
   Wood scrapers we are playing,
   hear us dance and sing.

Make Castanets!

From Spain

Castanets originate from the flamenco style of music and dance in the Andalusian region of Spain. Flamenco dancers hold castanets in their hands and play them as they stamp their feet and move their arms in the air while dancing. They click the castanets together by tapping one castanet against the other using their wrists and fingertips. Flamenco dance is very beautiful. The sharp clicking sound of the castanets helps the dancers keep the rhythm and makes the music exciting.

Castanets are traditionally made from wood and are connected together at one end with a leather lace. Your castanets will be made from cardboard, glue, and bottle caps. These recyclable models are even easier to play than the originals!

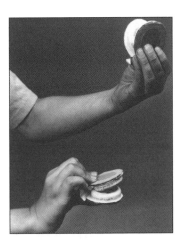

Time Needed: Two class periods—one for construction, one for decoration.

CRAFT SKILLS

- tracing
- cutting
- gluing
- bending
- painting

CONCEPTS

in between, center, together, around

MATERIALS NEEDED

- two 6 inch by 2 inch strips of corrugated cardboard
- two large bottle caps with smooth edges (such as juice or ice tea caps)
- white glue
- one pencil
- one pair of scissors
- one ruler or straight edge
- tempera paints and brushes

Make Castanets

1 👉 Trace or cut out the pattern for castanets from the *Appendix*.

2 👉 Place the pattern on top of your cardboard strip and trace it. Repeat this on a second piece of cardboard.

3 👉 Find the two dotted lines on the castanets pattern. Draw lines like these onto your cardboard strips in the same places.

👉 You can find these places by putting the pattern on the table right next to your cardboard strips. Place a ruler along one line on the pattern. Hold it there with one hand. Use your other hand to draw along the ruler's edge onto your cardboard strip. Do the same thing with the second line. *(See Figure 1.)*

4 Use a sharp pencil to press down on those lines in your cardboard. This makes a groove in the cardboard so it will bend in the proper places.

5 👉 Cut along the outer line you traced. This will make your strip into a castanet shell. *(See Figure 2.)*

6 Apply a lot of glue onto the inside edges of each bottle cap.

7 Pick up one bottle cap and press it, glue-side down, against the cardboard at one end of the castanets. Hold it there for the count of ten.

8 Take the other bottle cap and press it, glue-side down, against the cardboard at the opposite end of the castanets. Hold it there for the count of ten. Let the castanets dry overnight. (See Figure 3.)

9 When the glue is dry, you can paint the castanets! Use beautiful colors and paint designs on the cardboard tops and bottoms.

10 When the paint is dry, brush the outer flaps of the castanets with a coat of white glue. The glue will go on white, but will dry clear. This will make your castanets shiny and smooth, and protect the paint from flaking off. When the glue is dry, you are ready to play.

Figure 1

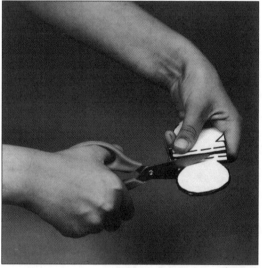

Figure 2

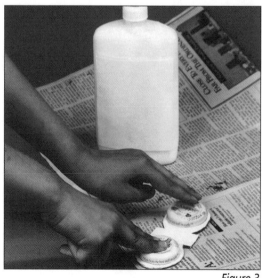

Figure 3

Play The Castanets

- Hold castanets in each hand. Rest the bottom flap of the castanets in your palm. Let the open end of the castanets rest on your fingers. *(See Figure 4.)*

- Lay your thumbs across the upper flaps of the castanets.

- Turn one hand over so that the backs of your fingers are pointing toward the sky and point one hand down toward the ground. *(See Figure 5.)*

- Play the castanets by tapping your fingertips together on the upper flaps of the castanets in time with the steady beat of the music.

Figure 4

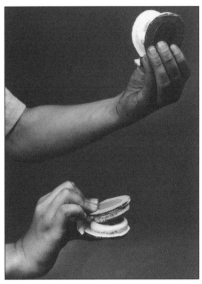

Figure 5

Read A Book

1. *Afro-Bets: Book Of Colors* (Pre K)
by Margaret Wise Brown (Just Us Books)
A rhyming poem takes readers through a variety of situations, helping children to identify six basic colors.

2. *Aunt Elaine Does The Dance From Spain* (Pre K-3)
by Leah Komaiko (Yearling)
Katy's favorite aunt, Elaine, loves to dress up in colorful costumes and become Elena, the Spanish dancer.

3. *The Story of Ferdinand* (Pre K-3)
by Manro Leaf (Viking)
This classic tale is about a peaceable bull who doesn't like to fight.

4. *What Color?* (Pre K)
Photos by Anthea Sieveking (Dial)
Children from a range of cultures, each dressed in a different color, are displayed in crisp photos, juxtaposed with colors of the color under consideration.

"My Eyes Are Smiling"
A Movement Activity Using American Sign Language and the Castanets

This lyric lends itself easily to American Sign Language. This is an opportunity to ask children how they would communicate if they could not hear. You can educate them by asking them how they think hearing-impaired people speak. Explain to your children that hearing-impaired people communicate with their hands, body-language, and facial expressions, and by reading people's lips. Together, you and the children can make music that hearing-impaired people and hearing people alike can enjoy.

Many hearing people find the act of signing to be a powerful experience, one that opens the heart and allows for a sense of unity with all people. If you have ever tried this activity with young people, you know how much children enjoy signing and how quickly they learn the signs.

Using this song, children can learn the signs for many different words, as well as the universal sign for "I love you." Just follow the pictures that follow to learn how to form the correct signs.

If you recite the words first using your voice and your hands, the children can copy you. While half the children sign, have the others accompany them on the castanets to maintain a steady beat. Then have them switch roles. After a few times of signing and singing the song, invite one or two children to stand with you facing the group so that they can lead other children in performing the signs. Almost everyone will want their turn being a leader, so practicing and learning the signs become an activity all its own!

My   *hands*   *are*   *open*

they're waving at you.   *They snap*   *and they clap*   *and they say*   *"I love you."*

My   *arms*   *are*   *open*

they're reaching for you.   *They hug*   *and they snuggle,*   *and they say*   *"I love you."*

37

My Eyes Are Smiling

(Verse based on the music of "Tus Ojos")

Music Adaptation, New Music and New Lyric by Jessica Baron Turner
and Ronny Schiff

Moderate Waltz

1. My eyes are brown and they're smil-ing at you. They
2. My eyes are blue and they're smil-ing at you. They
3. My eyes are green and they're smil-ing at you. They
4. My eyes are ha-zel, they're smil-ing at you. They

blink, they wink, they say "I love you." My eyes are brown and they're
blink, they wink, they say "I love you." My eyes are blue and they're
blink, they wink, they say "I love you." My eyes are green and they're
blink, they wink, they say "I love you." My eyes are ha-zel, they're

To Coda

smil-ing at you. They blink, they wink, they say, "I love you."
smil-ing at you. They blink, they wink, they say, "I love you."
smil-ing at you. They blink, they wink, they say, "I love you."
smil-ing at you. They blink, they wink, they

Chorus

My eyes, my eyes, my eyes are smil-ing at

you. Your eyes, your eyes, your eyes

1., 2.

3.

D.S. al Coda

are smil-ing, too. too.

CODA

say, "I love you."

Make A Buzz Disk!

From England

Buzz disks made with wooden disks were found in many areas such as in South America and South Africa. With their strange buzzing sound, they were used in rituals.

In England, where there is a long history of children's singing games and rhymes tied into education as well as play, buzz disks were made with string and cardboard for fun.

Time Needed: Two class periods—one for construction, one for decoration.

CRAFT SKILLS

- tracing
- stringing
- gluing
- bending
- stringing
- winding
- pulling

CONCEPTS

toward, away, fast, slow, hard, gentle, loud, soft

VOCABULARY

comb (honeycomb)—the place in the hive where the bees make honey

dew—small drops of water

nectar—a sweet juice that flowers make and bees collect to make honey

scone—a type of bun

MATERIALS NEEDED

- two thick coated paper plates
- two 16-inch pieces of string
- single-hole punch
- pen or pencil
- marking pens

Make A Buzz Disk!

1 ☞ Trace or cut out the pattern for the buzz disk from the *Appendix*.

2 Put your paper plates together, one on top of the other.

3 Place the pattern on top of your paper plates and trace it. *(See Figure 1.)*

4 Cut out the buzz disk shape by cutting along the line you traced. *(See Figure 2.)*

5 ☞ Using the single hole punch, or a sharp pencil, punch holes in each of the designated spots on the buzz disk pattern.

6 ☞ Place the pattern back on the buzz disk. Using your pencil, make a dot through each hole in the pattern. This will mark the spots on the buzz disk that also need holes punched into them. *(See Figure 3.)*

7 Use your hole punch to make a hole in each marked spot on your buzz disk. There should be two holes close to the center of the buzz disk, and four holes closer to its edge.

8 Now that your holes are punched, you can decorate your buzz disk with markers. Decorate both of the smooth sides. When you string the buzz disk, these two plates will face back to back instead of facing in the same direction. The traditional buzz disk pattern featured here creates a wonderful sight when the buzz disk is played.

Figure 1

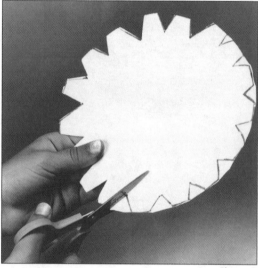

Figure 2

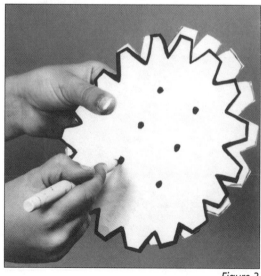

Figure 3

9 ☞ Now it is time to string your buzz disk. This is best done by an adult. Begin by picking up a string and threading one end of it into one center hole, and the other end into the other center hole. Close to the plate, tie the two together in an overhand knot, as if you were knotting two shoelaces. Now pick up the other string and do the same thing in the opposite direction on the buzz disk. When this whole process is complete, you should see two strings on each side of the buzz disk. *(See Figure 4.)*

10 Finally, for extra playing control, thread each string back through its center hole. All four strings will trade sides one last time. In the end, you will still have two strings on each side. Tie the loose ends on each side together in another overhand knot.

11 To make a greater humming sound, gently bend each triangle on the buzz disk away from the center of the instrument. Your buzz disk will look like two sunflowers with their petals facing away from one another. Now you are ready to play. *(See Figure 5.)*

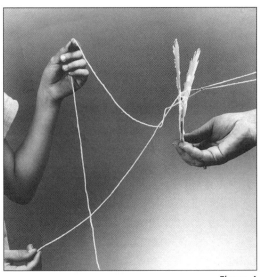

Figure 4

Figure 5

Play The Buzz Disk

- Grasp the strings on each side of the buzz disk in your hands. Your hands should be about six inches from the buzz disk and the buzz disk should be perpendicular to the ground. *(See Figure 6.)*

- Hold the strings tightly in each hand and twirl the buzz disk away from you, around and around. Wind it away from you until the strings are tightly wound. *(See Figure 7.)*

- Now pull your hands evenly away from the center as fast as you can. The buzz disk will unwind and make a soft whirring sound, like the wings of humming birds. *(See Figure 8.)*

Figure 6

Figure 7

Figure 8

Read A Book

1. *Anno's Britain* (Pre K-2)
by Mitsumasa Anno
A wordless picture book that brilliantly guides the "reader" through Britain.

2. *The Bee's Sneeze* (Pre K-1)
by Ellis Nadler (Simon and Schuster)
The fanciful story of a bee that has to sneeze.

3. *Madeline In London* (K-3)
by Ludwig Bemelman (Puffin)
Madeline's adventures in London.

4. *The Reason For A Flower* (Gr. 2-4)
by Ruth Heller (Grosset)
Rich illustrations and informative text focus especially on the interdependence of plants and animals.

5. *The Tiny Seed* (Pre K-2)
by Eric Carle (Picture Book Studios)
Brilliant collage illustrations take the seed through its life cycle and through the seasons.

Handy Dandy Riddledy Row
A Listening Activity Based On A Traditional English Rhyme

1. Players form a circle and one player stands in the center holding a buzz disk.

2. The players in the circle chant this rhyme:

   Handy dandy riddledy row
   will you pull it fast or slow?
   Handy dandy riddledy rye
   will you pull it low or high?

3. When the rhyme is over, the player in the center winds the buzz disk. Then he or she calls out one word (*fast, slow, high,* or *low*). This tells the group how he or she will pull on the strings of the buzz disk. The player proceeds to play the buzz disk as called.

4. When the buzz disk stops, the player joins the other children in the circle and a new player steps into the center. Once again, the group recites the rhyme and the center player chooses one way to play the buzz disk.

5. The game is over when everyone who wishes to play the buzz disk has had a turn.

In The Garden (Buzz, Buzz, Honey Bee)

(Based on the music of "Baa, Baa, Black Sheep")

Music Adaptation and New Lyric by
Jessica Baron Turner

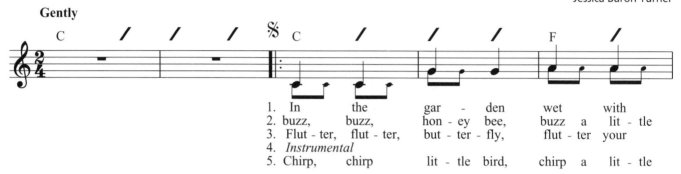

1. In the gar - den wet with
2. buzz, buzz, hon - ey bee, buzz a lit - tle
3. Flut - ter, flut - ter, but - ter - fly, flut - ter your
4. *Instrumental*
5. Chirp, chirp lit - tle bird, chirp a lit - tle

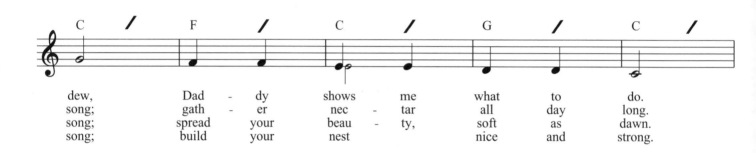

dew, Dad - dy shows me what to do.
song; gath - er nec - tar all day long.
song; spread your beau - ty, soft as dawn.
song; build your nest nice and strong.

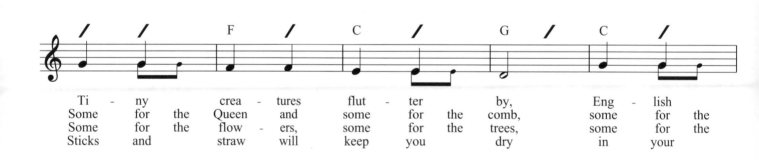

Ti - ny crea - tures flut - ter by, Eng - lish
Some for the Queen and some for the comb, some for the
Some for the flow - ers, some for the trees, some for the
Sticks and straw will keep you dry in your

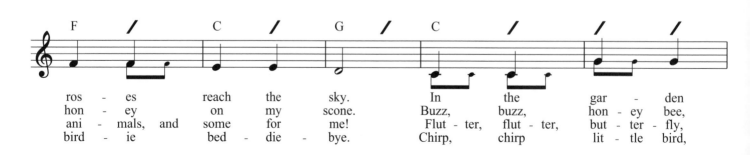

ros - es reach the sky. In the gar - den
hon - ey on my scone. Buzz, buzz, hon - ey bee,
ani - mals, and some for me! Flut - ter, flut - ter, but - ter - fly,
bird - ie bed - die - bye. Chirp, chirp lit - tle bird,

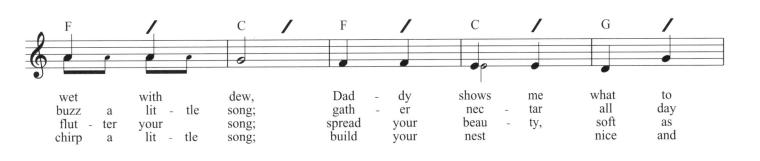

wet   with   dew,   Dad - dy   shows   me   what   to
buzz   a   lit - tle   song;   gath - er   nec - tar   all   day
flut - ter   your   song;   spread your   beau - ty,   soft   as
chirp   a   lit - tle   song;   build your   nest   nice   and

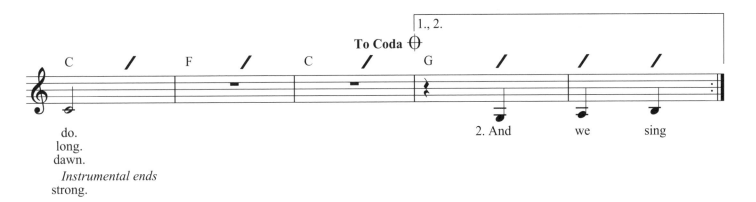

do.
long.
dawn.
Instrumental ends
strong.

2. And   we   sing

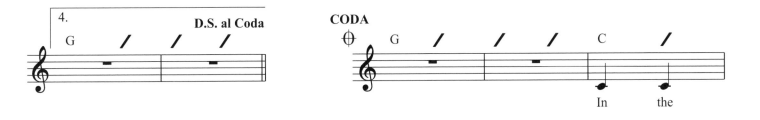

In   the

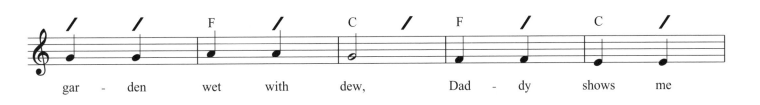

gar - den   wet   with   dew,   Dad - dy   shows   me

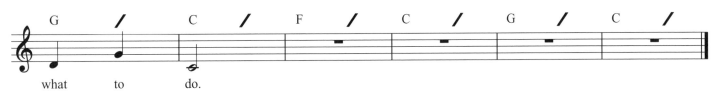

what   to   do.

For Cliff and Maureen Woods

Make Sleigh Bells!

From Germany & Austria

Sleigh bells are jingle bells and were originally worn by horses! They were attached to the horses' bridles so the horses made music as they pranced along pulling a sleigh. The bells let people know that horses were coming down the path or road. In Germany and Austria, the sleigh bells are associated with wintertime. Austrian composers such as Mozart and Mahler loved sleigh bells so much that they included them in their compositions.

Sleigh bells are easy to make. Just buy a package of jingle bells at your local hobby shop and string them together.

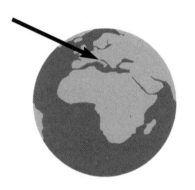

Time Needed: Two class periods—one for making beads (optional), one for construction

CRAFT SKILLS

- tying a knot
- stringing beads

CONCEPTS

up, down, shake, right, left, changing direction

VOCABULARY

prancing—a springy step that horses do
sleigh—a vehicle mounted on runners for use on snow or ice, usually pulled by a horse

MATERIALS NEEDED

- 16 small or eight large jingle bells
- 24 inches of thin plastic lanyard or lacing
- sixteen and one-half inch long beads or rigatoni noodles (see page 51)
- scissors

Make Sleigh Bells!

1. ☞ Tie a knot at one end of your lanyard or lacing.

2. ☞ Slide the lanyard or lacing through a bead and let the bead drop down to the knot at the bottom. Tie a knot around the bead. That bead will keep all your other beads and bells from falling off the end. *(See Figure 1.)*

3. Thread the lanyard or lacing through a jingle bell and pull the bell down to the bottom. Now slip another bead over the lanyard or lacing. Put the beads in between the bells for the best possible sound. Keep threading bells and beads until your thread is almost full. *(See Figure 2.)*

4. ☞ When you have only three inches of lanyard or lacing left, tie the two ends together in an overhand knot around the first bead you strung. Now trim the ends. Your sleigh bells are ready to play. You may wish to make sleigh bells for both hands. *(See Figure 3.)*

Figure 1

Figure 2

Figure 3

Play The Sleigh Bells

- Slip one hand inside a loop of sleigh bells. Let it drape over the palm of that hand.

- Now close your fingers over the sleigh bells to hold them in place. *(See Figure 4.)*

- To play the bells, simply move your hand up and down by bending your arm at the elbow or by bending at the wrist. Which way sounds and feels best to you?

Figure 4

Prancing Ponies
A Movement Activity for Sleigh Bells

1. While the children are learning to recite the words of "Prancing Ponies," have them hold the sleigh bells in their hands and shake them to the steady beat along with the recording.

2. As soon as they know the words, ask them to stand in a circle. Join them in the circle and explain that this time, in addition to shaking their sleigh bells, they can gallop around in a circle to the right. Before you begin, help them all face in the correct direction. This is a good opportunity to help the children establish a clear sense of direction. Before you play the recording, tell them, "This will help you put the beat in your feet." Lead the galloping, and model the motion and beat for the group!

3. When the children are moving well to the right, say "Change directions!" They may need help making an about face at ages three or four. By age five, this should come easily.

4. Now the children are ready to sing the song and play along!

Read A Book

1. ***The Elves and the Shoemaker*** (All ages)
   A traditional German folk tale available from many different publishers.

2. ***Fox's Dream*** (K-3)
   by Tejima (Philomel)
   A solitary fox on a snowy winter's night has an exciting chase.

3. ***The Pied Piper of Hamelin*** (Pre K-2)
   Illustrated by Mercer Mayer (Macmillan)
   A delightful traditional German tale.

4. ***The Snowman*** (Pre K)
   by Raymond Briggs (Random Books)
   A wordless picture book about a boy who builds a snowman that comes to life in his dreams.

5. ***The Snowy Day*** (K-3)
   by Ezra Jack Keats (Viking)
   A little boy named Peter explores his neighborhood on a snowy day.

Prancing Ponies

(Based on the music of "O, How Lovely Is The Evening" ["O, Wie Wohl Ist's Mir Am Abend"])

Music Adaptation and New Lyric by
Jessica Baron Turner

Moderate Waltz

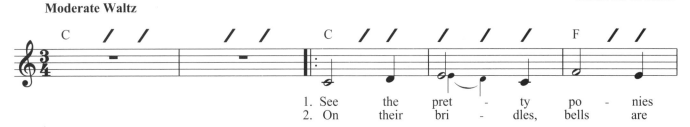

1. See the pret - ty po - nies
2. On their bri - dles, bells are

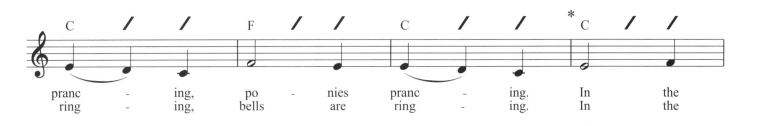

pranc - ing, po - nies pranc - ing. In the
ring - ing, bells are ring - ing. In the

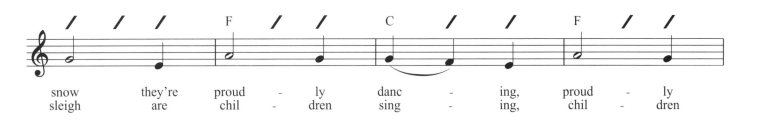

snow they're proud - ly danc - ing, proud - ly
sleigh are proud chil - dren sing - ing, proud chil - dren

Repeat and Fade
(after 2nd time)

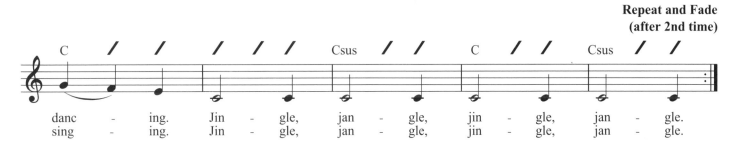

danc - ing. Jin - gle, jan - gle, jin - gle, jan - gle.
sing - ing. Jin - gle, jan - gle, jin - gle, jan - gle.

* To perform as a round, start the round here entering with the first verse during the second verse.

Make A Shekere!

From Nigeria

In Africa and Cuba, shekeres (*shaker-ā*) are made from large hollow gourds. First the gourd is dried and its top is cut off. This gives it an open mouth, like that of a jar. The gourd might be painted or stained. Then, beads are strung around the outside, starting from around its neck like a necklace. More beads are strung from the "necklace" down to another "necklace" around the base of the gourd. Those beads between the top and bottom are knotted together in beautiful patterns.

Shekeres originally come from the Yoruba people in Nigeria, Africa. There the shekeres are used, often to accompany drums, in special ceremonies and dances. People brought the shekere from Nigeria to Cuba, and today the shekere is played in Cuban music too.

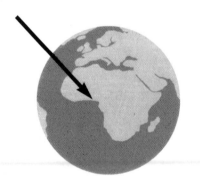

Time Needed: Two class periods—one period to make the rigatoni beads (optional), one period for construction.

CRAFT SKILLS

- twisting the ends of pipe cleaners around each other
- stringing beads
- making patterns with beads
- simple knot tying (this can be done by the adult)
- tucking string
- painting and dyeing beads (*optional*)

CONCEPTS

circle, diagonal, differences, hard, hollow, loud, patterns, quiet, round, sameness, shake, slap, through, under, high, low

MATERIALS NEEDED

- one large plastic bottle with a flat bottom
- two yards of lanyard or fishing line
- large beads
- four pipe cleaners
- buttons (*optional*)
- jingle bells (*optional*)

OPTIONAL RIGATONI BEADS
- rigatoni pasta
- food coloring
- denatured rubbing alcohol
- paper towels
- bowls or containers

Rigatoni Bead-Making Directions

This will take you less than fifteen minutes to do, *not* including stirring or drying time. However, it will take a day for the rigatoni beads to dry.

1. 👉 Place the food colorings on a piece of paper towel and open them.

2. 👉 For each color of rigatoni you wish to make, you need a separate container. Pour a half cup of denatured rubbing alcohol into each container.

3. 👉 Squirt several drops of each color into its own bowl of rubbing alcohol. Stir well. Add more food coloring for darker or brighter colors, less for lighter, pastel colors. *(See Figure 1.)*

4. Add rigatoni to each container and stir. Food coloring soaks into skin, so use rubber gloves or a stirring utensil to cover the rigatoni with the liquid. Children can assist in this task. *(See Figure 2.)*

5. Soak the rigatoni for at least an hour, turning every fifteen minutes for deep, even coverage.

6. 👉 When the rigatoni has reached the desired shade, remove it from the container and place it on paper toweling or newspaper to dry. Once dry, your rigatoni beads are ready to use. *(See Figure 3.)*

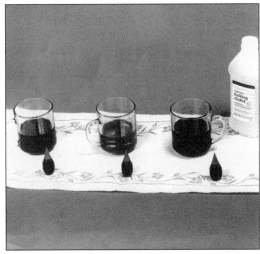

Figure 1

Figure 2

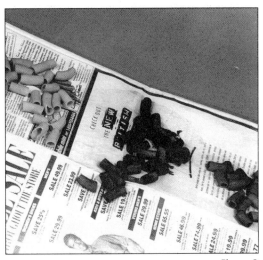

Figure 3

Make A Shekere

If you can make this project over a two or three day period of time, you can create more elaborate instruments.

1 ☞ First, choose or make your beads. You may wish to use just rigatoni beads or combine them with commercially-made beads or buttons. Alternating colors and shapes, or stringing beads and buttons in patterns will make your shekere more interesting to see and to hear.

2 ☞ If you use commercially-made beads or buttons, find large ones. Children will be stringing at least 40 big beads and this can easily take a half hour. Ask children to help you sort the big beads into one pile and the smaller ones into another pile. Show them examples of each kind before they begin. *(See Figure 4.)*

3 ☞ Next you will need the clean, dry plastic bottle and the pipe cleaners. Wrap a pipe cleaner, end to end, around the top portion or neck of the container to make the necklace. If you wish, this can be beaded.

4 ☞ Twist the ends together so that the pipe cleaner fits the neck of the container, but not too tightly. If you can fit one finger between the necklace and the container, the size is perfect. *(See Figure 5.)*

5 ☞ Repeat the same process around the base of the container, using two or more pipe cleaners twisted end to end. Fit the bottom necklace just like the top one. Be sure it sits above the bottom of the container and doesn't touch the table when you set the shekere down. *(See Figure 6.)*

6 ☞ Now you are ready to bead the shekere. Elaborate knotting is not necessary. Making straight rows of beads between the top and bottom necklaces will look and sound fine. Give each child a long piece of string or fishing line (a yard should suffice). Help them tie one end to the bottom "necklace." Make a double knot for them shere before they begin beading.

Figure 4

Figure 5

Figure 6

7 👉 Show the children how to string beads on the string by holding one end of it up in the air and feeding it through a few beads. You may want to demonstrate for them how to make a pattern with their beads. Then let them take over the beading. *(See Figure 7.)*

Figure 7

8 👉 When the children's strings have enough beads to span the distance between the bottom and top "necklaces," show them how to tuck their string under the top pipe cleaner and lead it over to continue beading. Again, the trick here is to leave the string a bit loose so it can slap freely against the container when shaken. A very tight string will stay rigidly in place and make very little sound. *(See Figure 8.)*

9 👉 Continue beading and looping your way around the shekere. This method will create a zig-zag around the entire container. The more string you bead, the closer together the zigs and zags will be.

Figure 8

10 👉 If your piece of string runs out, just add a new piece by tying it on at the end of the old one.

11 👉 When the string and beads reach the place where your beading began, tie it tightly to the closest "necklace." A double knot will help it keep its place during years of rigorous playing of the shekere. Now you are ready to play! *(See Figure 9.)*

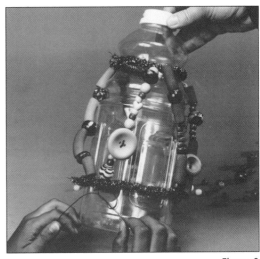

Figure 9

Play The Shekere

You can make three different sounds with your shekere…

1. First, hold your shekere by wrapping one hand around its neck. Now open your other hand and slap the shekere down into the flat palm of that hand. Listen to the sound that escapes through the mouth of the shekere! *(See Figure 10.)*

Figure 10

2. Place your open palm firmly across the bottom of the shekere, and keep your other hand around its neck. Now rock the shekere between your left hand and your right hand.

   Rock it toward your body and away from your body. *(See Figure 11.)*

   Listen to the beads clicking against the gourd or bottle! Do you hear a clickety-clack sound?

Figure 11

3. Hold the shekere against your body in the crook of your arm.

   Now open the palm of your free hand and slap it down over the mouth of the shekere. *(See Figure 12.)*

   Repeat this motion, but this time, do not cover the mouth of the shekere. Just slap the rim around the mouth.

   Does this sound different than when you covered up the mouth of the shekere? Practice slapping your palm over the mouth in different ways and you'll be able to make many new sounds, high and low.

Figure 12

Who Gives Comfort?
A Discussion and Movement Activity for the Shekere

1. Discuss the meaning of the word "comfort."

2. Ask children to name a person, place, or thing that gives them comfort when they feel sad, mad, or lonely. Give an example such as, "When I need comfort, I talk to a good friend."

3. Young children often want to be like their parents. Ask them to think about the ways their parents give them comfort. Encourage them to show the different ways *they* can give comfort to somebody else, like their parents do.

4. When the children begin to learn the song "Take Comfort Here," ask them to show you how they hold a baby. Next, show them how to rock the baby to the steady beat from side to side. As children learn to sing each line in response to the leader on the recording, encourage them to rock their babies while singing the song and telling their babies where to get comfort.

5. When the children have learned the song, introduce the shekere part. They can play the shekere on the count of *1-2-3-4* using the first or third playing method in the section called "PLAY THE SHEKERE."

6. This is a classic "call and response" song. Divide the children into two groups. Have one group "call" the verses out while the other group "responds" by singing the chorus.

7. After children have learned all of the verses and the chorus, help them put the movements and rhythms together. Divide them into two groups. One group can "rock their babies," while the others play the shekere.

Read A Book

1. A Is For Africa (Ages K-3)
by Ifeoma Onyefulu (Dutton)
These photos taken from Nigeria represent the warm family ties that are found in traditional village life.

2. A Country Far Away (Ages 3-6)
by Nigel Gray (Orchard)
Shows the similarities and differences between a boy in a rural African village and a western boy.

3. Families: Poems Celebrating the African-American Experience (Gr. 2-5)
by Dorothy Strickland and Michael R. Strickland (Wordsong/Boyd Mills Press)
A celebration of the close relationships and diversity of African-American families.

4. I Am Eyes – Ni Macho (Ages 5-7)
by Nonny Horgrogian (Scholastic)
A small girl in Kenya observes everything around her and shows that curiosity is universal.

5. I Love My Family (Ages 3-7)
by Wade Hudson (Scholastic)
Shows the warmth of family.

6. It Takes A Village (Ages 4-8)
by Jane Cowen-Fletcher (Scholastic)
Depicts the close knit community life in Nigeria.

7. Joshua's Masai Mask (Ages 3-7)
by Dakari Hru (Lee and Low)
Joshua loves to play his Kalimba – a traditional African musical instrument.

8. Misoso – Once Upon a Time Tales from Africa (Pre K-3)
retold by Verna Aardema (Alfred Knopf)
From Angola to Zanzibar, twelve misoso stories, or "once upon a time" tales sure to enthrall with imitable humor and flair. Vibrant illustrations.

9. The Village of Round and Square Houses (Gr. 1-4)
by Ann Grifalconi (Little, Brown and Co.)
This Caldecott Honor Book tells the story of Tos — a village where women live in round houses and men live in square houses.

10. Where Are You Going Manyoni? (K-3)
by Catherine Stock (Morrow)
Manyoni sets out from her home near the Limpopo River in Zimbabwe to school. A great geography lesson and view of African childhood.

Take Comfort Here
(Concept based on "O, Do Not Cry")

Music and Lyric by
Jessica Baron Turner

Make A Frame Drum!

From Native America, The Sioux Nation

In the Native American cultures, frame drums are made from wooden frames with animal skins stretched over the frame and laced tightly into place with leather. The drums can make many beautiful sounds. Often drums were played in sacred ceremonies.

The frames are traditionally round, but some newer drums are made with many-sided frames. The Plains Indians, such as the Dakota Sioux who lived in the area of North and South Dakota, Minnesota, and Nebraska, are known for their laced-frame drums.

Time Needed: Two class periods—one for construction, one for decoration and mallet.

CRAFT SKILLS

- cutting cardboard and paper
- folding
- painting with glue
- taping
- threading
- knot tying

CONCEPTS

bottom, inside, outside, over, rectangle, square, tight, top, striking

MATERIALS NEEDED

FRAME DRUM

- one empty ice cream bucket or one square cardboard box with four flaps on both top and bottom
- one large paper grocery bag (plain)
- white glue
- one large paint brush for gluing
- smaller paintbrushes for painting
- three yards of string or yarn, cut into two equal lengths
- one-hole punch
- tape
- tempera paint

MALLET

- one stick about 12 inches long
- two old socks
- 12 inches of ribbon or yarn, or a rubber band, or hair tie

Make A Frame Drum!

1 ☞ If you are going to make a round drum, use a sharp knife or scissors to cut out a section of the ice cream bucket. Make the bucket at least five inches deep, without a top or bottom.

If you are making a square drum, fold in all four flaps of the box on the top and bottom. This will make a strong, open frame.

2 ☞ Cut a large brown paper bag down each side so you have a large sheet of paper that can completely cover over one end of the frame. Trace the frame on the brown paper. Leave two inches of paper hanging over the edges around the frame to make taping it down easier. *(See Figure 1.)*

3 ☞ Wipe the top of the paper only with a damp sponge, then pull the paper tightly over the frame and tape the dry edges down. *(See Figure 2.)*

4 When the paper dries, paint a design on it. This can be anything you like. You might wish to paint a picture of an animal or something else from nature. Next, allow the paint to dry.

5 ☞ When the paint is dry, spread a thick coat of glue onto the paper and brush it evenly across the entire surface. Let it dry completely. This glue will dry clear and make your drumhead taut and resonant, while allowing your painting to show through. *(See Figure 3.)*

6 When the glue is dry, turn the frame over. Now your box should be covered with paper on one end and open on the other. Spread glue all over the back of the paper inside the drum, just like you did on the top side of it. Let that dry, too.

7 ☞ Using your one-hole punch, make a hole in the middle of each side of the box for a square drum, or in the four opposite positions for a circular drum. *(See Figure 4.)*

8 ☞ Tie a large knot on one end of your string, so that it won't slip through the hole.

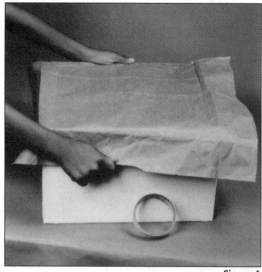

Figure 1

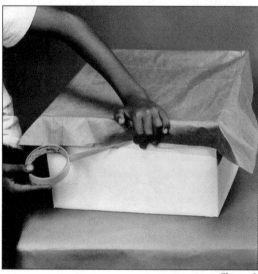

Figure 2

Figure 3

9   ☞ Thread the string through one hole and pull it across the frame to the hole opposite it. Then pull it through that hole, and tie another large knot. *(See Figure 4.)*

10   ☞ Repeat Step 9 with the next two holes. This lacing gives you a good way to hold the drum from behind.

Make The Mallet

1   Be sure your stick feels good to hold.

2   Place the toe of one sock over the top of the stick, then wrap the rest of the sock around the stick at the same end.

3   Now slide the other sock over the first one and unroll it. *(See Figure 5.)*

4   Tie a ribbon or piece of yarn around the outer sock just below the bulk made by the inner sock. *(See Figure 6.)*

5   ☞ Cut off the extra sock fabric one inch below the ribbon. Now you have a drum stick or mallet. *(See Figure 7.)*

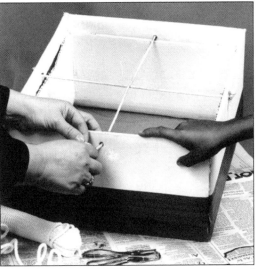

Figure 4

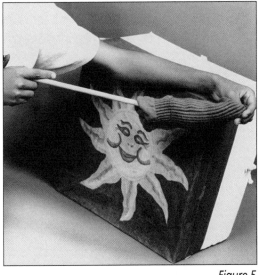

Figure 5

Figure 6

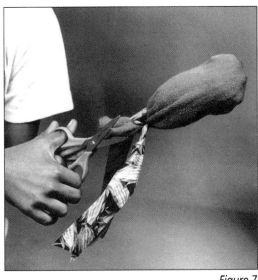

Figure 7

Play The Frame Drum

Figure 8

- Hold your drum by gripping the laces on the back in one hand.

- Hold the drum in front of your body with its head facing your other hand. This makes hitting the drum very easy. *(See Figure 8.)*

- You can play the frame drum two different ways.

  1. Hit the head of the drum with your open palm. Listen to the sound and find out how many new sounds you can create by hitting the drum in different ways. A higher sound comes from hitting it near the frame, and a lower one comes from hitting it in the middle. Play with just one finger at a time. Your drum can tell a story just using different parts of your hand! Can you make the drum play quietly? Loudly? Slowly? Quickly?

  2. Now play the drum with your mallet. Hold the mallet by placing the handle in the palm of your free hand and curling your fingers around it. Rest your thumb over your fingers, and bring the mallet down on the head of the drum. Can you make a nice big sound?

Read A Book

1. Dance of the Sacred Circle – A Native American Tale (Gr. 1-4)
Adapted by Kristina Rodanas (Little, Brown, and Co.) Inspired by a Blackfeet myth, this moving tale of bravery and magic tells of the journey of a young boy whose tribe is on the brink of starvation.

2. The First Strawberries – A Cherokee Story (Ages 4-8)
retold by Joseph Bruchac (Dial) This captivating Cherokee tale explains how strawberries came into the world.

3. The Girl Who Loved Horses (Gr. 1-4)
by Paul Goble (Bradbury Press) This Caldecott Award winner is an enchanting story of a Native American girl's love of horses.

4. Heetunka's Harvest – A Tale of the Plains Indians (Gr. 1-3)
retold by Jennifer Berry Jones (Roberts Rinehart Publishers) An authentic Native American legend about a Dakota woman who learned a hard lesson about greed and selfishness.

5. This Land Is My Land (Ages 4-8)
by George Littlechild (Children's Book Press) Highlights the struggles of Native Americans. Delightful stories of human healing.

The Horses Are Running
A Story Rhyme For The Frame Drum

In some places, wild horses run free. Sometimes these wild horses are called "mustangs." They run and stay together in bands. Their hooves upon the ground make a powerful sound. You can tell a story about these horses using your frame drum and this rhyme. Any number of people and players can join in.

Begin by asking children to think of some places where horses would run free. Ask if they have ever heard of a meadow. Show them a picture of a meadow or describe it to them. Now you are ready to rhyme and play.

In the beginning of the rhyme, when the horses are still far away, ask children to play their drums with just two fingers. As the horses get closer, encourage them to play louder and louder, until they are using entirely open hands on the frame drum.

When the horses run into town, instruct the children to hit the drum as loudly as they can to show that the horses are right there.

As the horses leave the town, remind children to play quieter. As the horses go over the hill and out to the meadow, lead the children in playing softer and softer and gently, until they are only using two fingers again.

When you all recite the words "quiet and still," play even softer, until the sound completely disappears!

Recite...

The horses are running and running and running;

the horses are coming over the hill.

The horses are running and running and running;

the horses are coming closer still!

The horses are running and running and running;

the horses are running into town.

There's a black one, there's a white one;

there's a grey one, there's a brown!

The horses are running and running and running;

the horses are running out of town.

There's a black one, there's a white one;

there's a grey one, there's a brown!

The horses are running and running and running;

the horses are going over the hill.

The horses are running to the meadow;

now our town is quiet and still!

Sweet, Sweet, We Have Food To Eat

(Based on the music of "Wanagi Wacipi Olowan" [Dakota Sioux])

Music Adaptation and New Lyric by
Jessica Baron Turner

Additional Lyrics

4. Sweet, sweet, we have greens to eat.
Sweet, sweet, we have greens to eat.
Greens to feed us all;
make us strong and tall.

5. Sweet, sweet, we have meat to eat.
Sweet, sweet, we have meat to eat.
Meat to feed us all;
make us strong and tall.

6. Sweet, sweet, we have food to eat.
Sweet, sweet, we have food to eat.
Food to feed us all;
make us strong and tall.
Food to feed us all;
make us strong and tall.

Let's Make Music Again!
Song and Activity for all of the Instruments

This activity gives everyone—children and adults—an opportunity to make music together using all of the instruments made from this book! The song helps everyone practice playing each instrument along with identifying the instruments' names, sounds, and countries of origin. The activity can be done solo by one child or by a group.

You will need a floor space large enough to allow the players to sit in a circle with their instruments spread before them.

1. For a group, invite all the players to sit in the circle, and then place an instrument in front of each person in the order of the countries on the recording. Begin with the maracas and end with the frame drum.

   Or each player can bring all of his or her instruments to the circle and spread them out on the floor. Begin with the maracas on the far left and end with the frame drum on the far right.

2. Explain to the players that they can sing and play along with the song. If they are playing only one instrument, they should wait for their turn and play their instrument when the country is called.

   If they are playing all of their instruments, when they hear the name of each new country they should pick up the instrument from that country and play along with the recording. When each verse is over, they should put down the instrument and wait to hear the name of the next instrument.

3. During the last verse of the song, players can choose their favorite instrument from the line and play it again!

Read A Book

1. *Aekung' Dream* (Pre K-3)
   by Min Paek (Children's Book Press)
   A little girl's poor English and different ways bring about taunts from classmates. Text is also Korean.

2. *All the Colors of the Earth* (All Ages)
   by Sheila Hamanaka (Morrow)
   This books celebrates the dazzling diversity of children.

3. *All the Colors of the Race* (Gr. 1-4)
   Illustrated by John Steptoe (Lothrop)
   A lyrical tribute to children everywhere.

4. *Count Your Way Through...* (Gr. 1-4)
   by Jim Haskins (Carolrhoda Books)
   This series of counting books includes titles focusing on Africa (Swahili), Arabia, Canada (French), China, Germany, India, Japan, Korea, Mexico, and Russia.

5. *Everybody Cooks Rice* (Ages 4-8)
   by Norah Dooley (Carolrhoda Books)
   Carrie learns that people in her neighborhood are from different cultures but that everyone cooks rice dishes.

6. *Fathers, Mothers, Sisters, Brothers: A Collection of Family Poems* (Pre K-2)
   by Marilyn Hafner (Little, Brown, and Co.)
   26 poems celebrating family types and ethnic backgrounds.

7. *How My Family Lives In America* (Gr. 1-4)
   by Susan Kuklin (Bradbury)
   Family cultures are described through the eyes of an African-American girl, a Latino boy, and a Chinese-American girl.

8. *Jamaica and Brianna* (Pre K-1)
   by Anne Sibley O'Brien (Houghton Mifflin)
   Arguments between an African-American girl and a Asian-American girl teach about jealousy in friendship.

9. *My Song Is Beautiful – Poems and Pictures in Many Voices* (Ages 4 and up)
   selected by Mary Ann Hoberman (Little, Brown, and Co.)
   Fourteen poems written from the perspective of varied cultures, all emphasize the common hopes and dreams that all children share.

10. *People* (Pre K-6)
    by Peter Spier (Doubleday)
    A charming and fun book with an inspiring message, not simply about the right to be different, but about the excitement of difference.

Let's Make Music Again

Music and Lyric by
Jessica Baron Turner

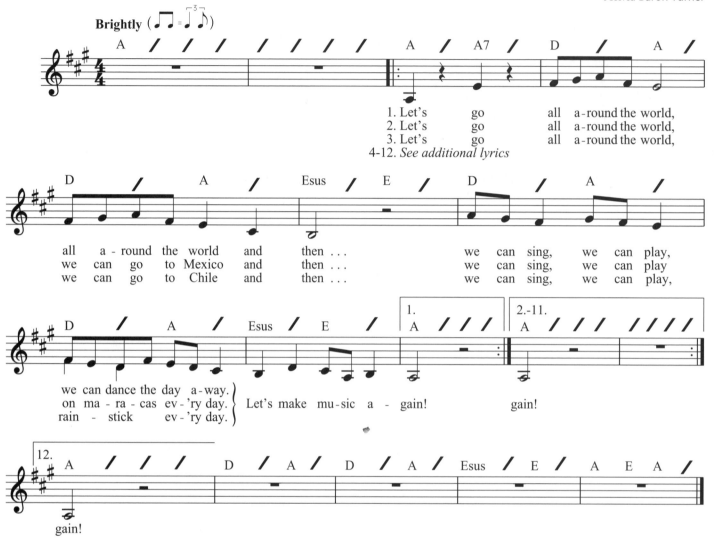

Additional Lyrics

4. Let's go all around the world,
   go to Australia and then...
   we can sing, we can play
   wood clappers every day.
   Let's make music again!

5. Let's go all around the world,
   we can go to China and then...
   we can sing, we can play
   pien chung every day.
   Let's make music again!

6. Let's go all around the world,
   we can go to India and then...
   we can sing, we can play
   wood scraper every day.
   Let's make music again!

7. Let's go all around the world,
   we can go to Spain and then...
   we can sing, we can play
   castanets every day.
   Let's make music again!

8. Let's go all around the world,
   we can go to England and then...
   we can sing, we can play
   buzz disk every day.
   Let's make music again!

9. Let's go all around the world,
   we can go to Germany and then...
   we can sing, we can play
   jingle bells every day.
   Let's make music again!

10. Let's go all around the world,
    go to Nigeria and then...
    we can sing, we can play
    shekere every day.
    Let's make music again!

11. Let's go all around the world,
    to the Sioux nation and then...
    we can sing, we can play
    frame drum every day.
    Let's make music again!

12. Let's go all around the world,
    all around the world and then...
    we can sing, we can play
    we can dance the day away.
    Let's make music again!

Recycled Materials And Resource Guide

Material	Where To Find It
Plastic bottles:	• dentist's offices (mouthwash) • restaurants (dressings, sauces) • laundromats (detergent) • pre-schools (juice and milk containers)
Seeds and Pebbles:	• parks, backyard, and nature preserves • hardware stores and garden shops • beaches (sand, pebbles and seashells)
Tubes:	• giftshops (used wrapping paper tubes) • carpet stores • poster stores • Post Office • copy shops (used drafting paper tubes) • plastic's supply stores (clear tubing)
Wooden Stirrers/Tongue Depressors:	• doctor's offices • craft stores and hobby shops • lumber yards and paint stores • hardware stores
Bottle Caps with Smooth Edges:	• bottling companies • recycling companies • school cafeterias • convenience stores • neighbors' houses • sporting events/venues
Cardboard/chipboard— corrugated and thin:	• grocery/convenience stores • pharmacies • appliance stores • bookstores • dry cleaners • art supply stores
Jingle Bells:	• craft and hobby stores • fabric stores • variety stores • Christmas stores/decorations
Buttons and Beads:	• thrift and resale shops • old clothing • fabric stores • craft and hobby stores • bead stores
Ice Cream Barrels:	• ice cream and yogurt shops • variety stores

Tracing Patterns

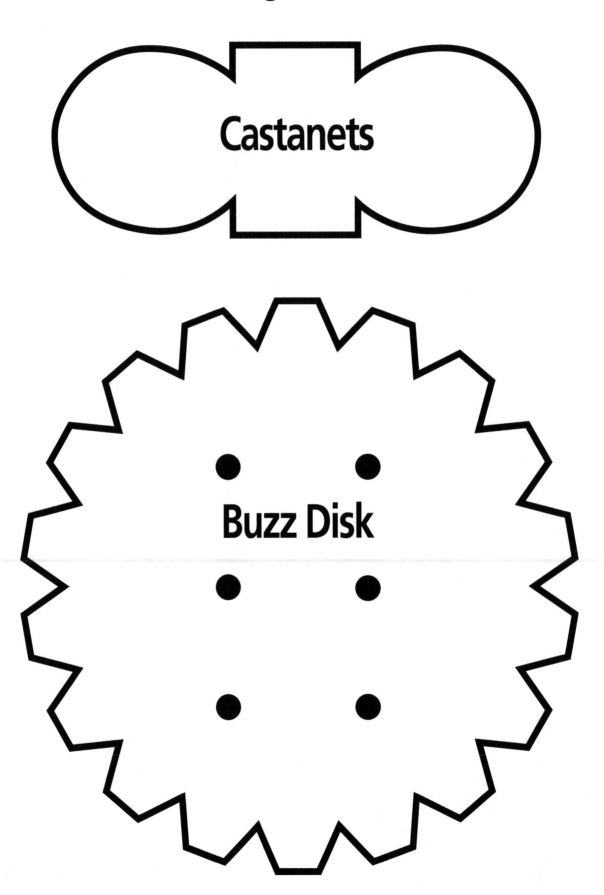

Castanets

Buzz Disk

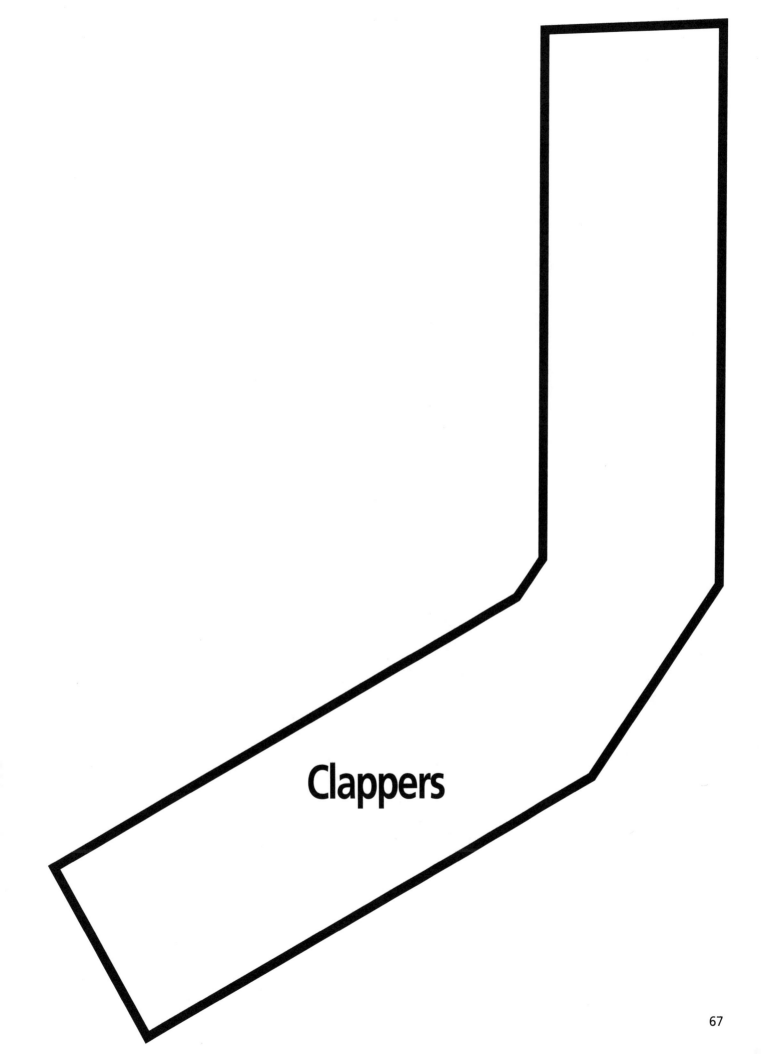

Clappers

Photographs of the Authentic Instruments

Castanets

Maracas

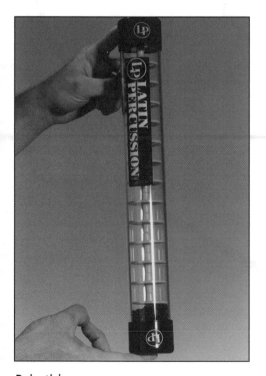

Rainstick

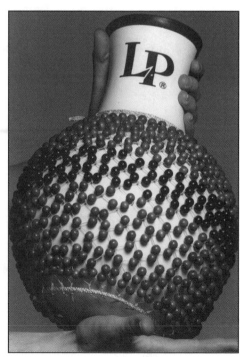

Shekere

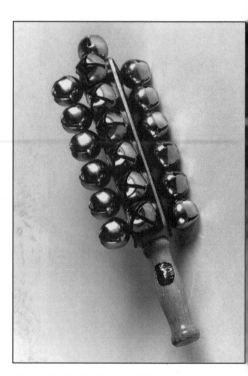

Jingle Bells (Sleigh Bells)

Photographs on this page courtesy of Latin Percussion Music Group.

Frame Drum

Pien Chung (Temple Bells)

Photographs on this page courtesy of Mid-East Manufacturing, Inc.

LET'S MAKE MUSIC
Recording Credits

Dimas Arellanos	trumpet
Jon Baker	wood clappers
Matt Cartsonis	accordian
Joachim Cooder	percussion
Gino D'Auri	flamenco guitars
Scott Danforth	vocals, spoken word
Arnie Gomez	vocals
Edgar Gomez	vocals
M.B. Gordy	percussion
Justin Jackson	vocals
"Brother Bru Bru" Bruce Langhorn	MIDI & sound design
George Llanes	guitarron, guitar
Dorian Michael	steel string guitar, mandolin
Jerry Moore	vocals
Tom Nolan	vocals
Marvin Sanders	sound design
Ronny Susan Schiff	percussion, vocals
Christine Schillinger	vocals
Laurie Schillinger	vocals
Mark Schillinger	vocals
Martin Simpson	guitar, vocals
David Trasoff	sarod, tamboura
Jessica Baron Turner	guitar, percussion, synth, vocals
Carmen Twillie	vocals
Danielle Weiner	vocals
Sabrina Weiner	vocals
David Zasloff	shakuhachi

Produced by Jessica Baron Turner
Engineered by Ira Ingber at Muscletone Music and
Andy Waterman and Jon Baker at The Bakery

Many thanks to Ry Cooder for his guidance during production...

Reproducible Lyric Sheets

These Are The Colors I Know
(Based on "Chiapanecas")
Music Adaptation and New Lyric by Jessica Baron Turner

Verse 1 Red is a color I know. Rojo!
Red as the roosters that crow. Rojo!
In Spanish we call it "rojo." Rojo!
Red is a color I know. Rojo!

Chorus 1 Red, red, red is a color,
bolder than every other.
Red, red, red is a color,
in Spanish we call it "rojo"! Rojo!

Verse 2 White is a color I know. Blanco!
White as the tortilla dough. Blanco!
In Spanish we call it "blanco." Blanco!
White is a color I know. Blanco!

Chorus 2 White, white, white is a color,
brighter than every other.
White, white, white is a color,
in Spanish we call it "blanco"! Blanco!

Red, red, red is a color,
bolder than every other
Red, red, red is a color,
in Spanish we call it "rojo"! Rojo!

Verse 3 Green is a color we say "verde."
Green as the chiles in May. Verde!
In Spanish we call it "verde." Verde!
Green is a color we say "verde."

Green, green, green is a color,
fresher than every other.
Green, green, green is a color,
in Spanish we call it "verde"! Verde!

Chorus 3 White, white, white is a color,
brighter than every other.
White, white, white is a color,
in Spanish we call it "blanco"! Blanco!

Red, red, red is a color,
bolder than every other.
Red, red, red is a color,
in Spanish we call it "rojo"! Rojo!

Verse 4 Red, white, and green are the colors,
waving like sisters and brothers.
Red, white, and green are the colors,
on the flag of Mexico.
Rojo, blanco, verde, olé!

Canta, Canta, Pretty Dove (Sing, Sing, Pretty Dove)

(based on "Canta, Canta, Pajarito")

Music Adaptation and New Lyric by Jessica Baron Turner

Verse 1　　Canta, canta, pajarito;
canta, canta, pretty dove.
Canta, canta, pajarito,
in the spring you sing a song of love.

Canta, canta, pajarito;
canta, canta, pretty dove.
Canta, canta, pajarito,
feel the raindrops falling from above.

Verse 2　　Canta, canta, pajarito;
canta, canta, pretty dove.
Canta, canta, pajarito,
in the spring you sing a song of love.

Canta, canta, pajarito;
canta, canta, cu, cu, ru.
Canta, canta, pajarito,
how the showers help the flowers bloom.

Verse 3　　Canta, canta, pajarito;
canta, canta, pretty dove.
Canta, canta, pajarito,
in the spring you sing a song of love.

Canta, canta, pajarito;
canta, canta, as you fly.
Canta, canta pajarito,
see the rainbow coloring the sky.

Reproducible Lyric Sheet

We'll Go A-Walking About In The Bush

(Based on "Craigielea")
Music Adaptation and New Lyric by Jessica Baron Turner

Chorus We'll go a-walking, we'll go a-walking,
we'll go a-walking about in the bush.
And it's hush, hush, hush,
listen to the animals,
while we're a-walking about in the bush.

Verse 1 Where's the koala, where's the koala,
where's the koala bear out in the bush?
He is chew, chew, chew, chew,
chewing eucalyptus leaves,
while we're a-walking about in the bush.

Chorus And we'll go a-walking,
we'll go a-walking, etc.

Verse 2 Where is the kanga, where is the kanga,
where is the kangaroo out in the bush?
She is jump, jump, jump, jump,
jumping with her joeys,
while we're out a-walking about
in the bush.

Chorus And we'll go a-walking,
we'll go a-walking, etc.

Verse 3 Where's kookaburra, where's kookaburra,
where's kookaburra bird out in the bush?
Well, he's haw, haw, haw, haw,
hawing with his family,
while we're a-walking about in the bush.

Chorus And we'll go a-walking,
we'll go a-walking,
we'll go a-walking about in the bush.
And it's hush, hush, hush,
listen to the animals,
while we're a-walking about in the bush.

Chan Mali Chew

(Based on "Can Mali Can")
Music Adaptation and New Lyric by Jessica Baron Turner & Paula Ravets

Verse 1   I have a baby goat.
He likes to chew
the buttons on your shirt
and the buckles on your shoe.
His mommy doesn't mind,
'cause she's a goat too.
Chan mali, chan mali, chan mali chew.

Chorus   Chan mali chan, *oi oi,*
chan mali chan, *oi oi.*
Chan mali, chan mali,
chan mali chew.
Chan mali chan, *oi oi,*
chan mali chan, *oi oi.*
Chan mali, chan mali,
chan mali chew.

Verse 2   I have a lucky bird,
she is a crane.
She has big wings
and a teeny tiny brain.
Her neck is like a noodle
and her legs are too.
Chan mali, chan mali, chan mali chew.

Chorus   Chan mali chan, *oi oi,*
chan mali chan, *oi oi.*
Chan mali, chan mali,
chan mali chew.
Chan mali chan, *oi oi,*
chan mali chan, *oi oi.*
Chan mali, chan mali,
chan mali chew.

Verse 3   I have a shiny fish,
it is a koi.
It gurgles like a girl,
but it bubbles like boy.
We don't know what to name it,
so we call it Billy Sue.
Chan mali, chan mali, chan mali chew.

Chorus   Chan mali chan, *oi oi,*
chan mali chan, *oi oi.*
Chan mali, chan mali,
chan mali chew.
Chan mali chan, *oi oi,*
chan mali chan, *oi oi.*
Chan mali, chan mali,
chan mali chew.

Verse 4   I have a furry panda,
he kisses and he hugs.
He looks a lot like Grandma,
but he likes to play with bugs.
He washes in the water
and he brushes with bamboo.
Chan mali, chan mali, chan mali chew.

Chorus   Chan mali chan, *oi oi,*
chan mali chan, *oi oi.*
Chan mali, chan mali,
chan mali chew.
Chan mali chan, *oi oi,*
chan mali chan, *oi oi.*
Chan mali, chan mali,
chan mali chew.

Reproducible Lyric Sheet

We Dance With Love

(Based on "Dancing With Gourds")
Music Adaptation and New Lyric by Jessica Baron Turner

Verse 1   We play with scrapers and with sticks,
            here in India.
        Wood scrapers we are playing,
            hear us dance and sing.

Verse 2   We dance with jingles on our ankles,
            here in India.
        Jingles upon our ankles,
            hear us dance and sing.

Verse 3   We drum upon the pretty tablas,
            here in India.
        Drumming upon the tablas,
            hear us dance and sing.

Verse 4   We play for family and friends,
            here in India.
        For all our family,
            we love to dance and sing.

Verse 5   We dance with love inside our hearts,
            here in India.
        With love for everybody,
            hear us dance and sing.

Verse 6   We play with scrapers and with sticks,
            here in India.
        Wood scrapers we are playing,
            hear us dance and sing.
        Wood scrapers we are playing,
            hear us dance and sing.

My Eyes Are Smiling

(Based on "Tus Ojos")
Music Adaptation and New Lyric
by Jessica Baron Turner & Ronny Susan Schiff

Verse 1   My eyes are brown and
  they're smiling at you.
They blink, they wink,
  they say "I love you."
My eyes are brown and
  they're smiling at you.
They blink, they wink,
  they say "I love you."

Chorus   My eyes, my eyes, my eyes
  are smiling at you.
Your eyes, your eyes,
  your eyes are smiling, too.

Verse 2   My eyes are blue and
  they're smiling at you.
They blink, they wink,
  they say "I love you."
My eyes are blue and
  they're smiling at you.
They blink, they wink,
  they say "I love you."

Chorus...

Verse 3   My eyes are green and
  they're smiling at you.
They blink, they wink,
  they say "I love you."
My eyes are green and
  they're smiling at you.
They blink, they wink,
  they say "I love you."

Verse 4   My eyes are hazel,
  they're smiling at you.
They blink, they wink,
  they say "I love you."
My eyes are hazel,
  they're smiling at you.
They blink, they wink,
  they say "I love you."

Additional Verse Activities with Sign Language

My hands are open,
they're waving at you.
They snap and they clap, and
they say "I love you."

Repeat

My arms are open,
they're reaching for you.
They hug and they snuggle,
they say "I love you."

Repeat

Reproducible Lyric Sheet

In The Garden (Buzz, Buzz, Honey Bee)

(Based on "Baa, Baa, Black Sheep")
Music Adaptation and New Lyric by Jessica Baron Turner

Verse 1   In the garden wet with dew,
Daddy shows me what to do.
Tiny creatures flutter by,
English roses reach the sky.
In the garden wet with dew,
Daddy shows me what to do.

Verse 2   Buzz, buzz, honey bee,
  buzz a little song;
gather nectar all day long.
Some for the Queen,
  and some for the comb,
and some for the honey on my scone.
Buzz, buzz, honey bee,
  buzz a little song;
gather nectar all day long.

Verse 3   Flutter, flutter, butterfly,
  flutter your song;
spread your beauty, soft as dawn.
Some for the flowers,
  some for the trees,
some for the animals
  and some for me!
Flutter, flutter, butterfly,
  flutter your song;
spread your beauty, soft as dawn.

Verse 4   *Instrumental*

Verse 5   Chirp, chirp, little bird,
  chirp a little song;
build your nest nice and strong.
Sticks and straw will keep you dry
in your birdie beddie-bye.
Chirp, chirp, little bird,
  chirp a little song;
build your nest nice and strong.

End   In the garden wet with dew,
Daddy shows me what to do.

Reproducible Lyric Sheet

Prancing Ponies

(Based on "O, How Lovely Is The Evening" ["O Wie Wohl Ist's Mir Am Abend"])
Music Adaptation and New Lyric by Jessica Baron Turner

Verse 1 See the pretty ponies prancing,
ponies prancing.
In the snow they're proudly dancing,
proudly dancing.
Jingle, jangle, jingle, jangle.

Verse 2 On their bridles, bells are ringing,
bells are ringing.
In the sleigh are children singing,
children singing.
Jingle, jangle, jingle, jangle.

© 1995 Knobby Knees Music

Take Comfort Here

(Concept based on "O, Do Not Cry")
Music Adaptation and New Lyric by Jessica Baron Turner

Verse 1 Come to your mama,
take comfort here.
Come to your mama,
take comfort here.
Somebody loves you, yes I do.

Chorus Somebody loves you,
take comfort here.
Somebody loves you,
take comfort here.
Somebody loves you, yes I do.

Verse 2 Come to your papa,
take comfort here.
Come to your papa,
take comfort here.
Somebody loves you, yes I do.

Chorus Somebody loves you,
take comfort here.
Somebody loves you,
take comfort here.
Somebody loves you, yes I do.

Verse 3 Come to your sister,
take comfort here.
Come to your sister,
take comfort here.
Somebody loves you, yes I do.

Verse 4 Come to your brother,
take comfort here.
Come to your brother,
take comfort here.
Somebody loves you, yes I do.

Chorus Somebody loves you,
take comfort here.
Somebody loves you,
take comfort here.
Somebody loves you, yes I do.
Somebody loves you, yes I do.

Finale Your auntie loves you, yes I do
Your uncle loves you, yes I do.
Your cousin loves you, yes I do.
Your grandma loves you, yes I do.
Your grandpa loves you, yes I do.
Your teacher loves you, yes I do.
Your best friend loves you, yes I do.

© 1995 Knobby Knees Music

(Dedicated to Mary Anne Schenkkan)

Reproducible Lyric Sheet

Sweet, Sweet, We Have Food To Eat

(Based on the music of "Wanagi Wacipi Olowan" [Dakota Sioux])
Music Adaptation and New Lyric by Jessica Baron Turner

Chorus Sweet, sweet, we have food to eat.
Sweet, sweet, we have food to eat.
Food to feed us all;
make us strong and tall.

Verse 1 Sweet, sweet, we have corn to eat.
Sweet, sweet, we have corn to eat.
Corn to feed us all;
make us strong and tall.

Verse 2 Sweet, sweet, we have fruit to eat.
Sweet, sweet, we have fruit to eat.
Fruit to feed us all;
make us strong and tall.

Verse 3 Sweet, sweet, we have greens to eat.
Sweet, sweet, we have greens to eat.
Greens to feed us all;
make us strong and tall.

Verse 4 Sweet, sweet, we have meat to eat.
Sweet, sweet, we have meat to eat.
Meat to feed us all;
make us strong and tall.

Chorus Sweet, sweet, we have food to eat.
Sweet, sweet, we have food to eat.
Food to feed us all;
make us strong and tall.
Food to feed us all;
make us strong and tall.

Reproducible Lyric Sheet

Let's Make Music Again!

by Jessica Baron Turner

Verse 1 Let's go all around the world,
all around the world and then…
we can sing, we can play,
we can dance the day away.
Let's make music again!

Verse 2 Let's go all around the world,
we can go to Mexico and then…
we can sing, we can play
on maracas everyday.
Let's make music again!

Verse 3 Let's go all around the world,
we can go to Chile and then…
we can sing, we can play
rainstick everyday.
Let's make music again!

Verse 4 Let's go all around the world,
go to Australia and then…
we can sing, we can play
wood clappers everyday.
Let's make music again!

Verse 5 Let's go all around the world,
we can go to China and then…
we can sing, we can play
pien chung everyday.
Let's make music again!

Verse 6 Let's go all around the world,
we can go to India and then…
we can sing, we can play
wood scrapers everyday.
Let's make music again!

Verse 7 Let's go all around the world,
we can go to Spain and then…
we can sing, we can play
castanets everyday.
Let's make music again!

Verse 8 Let's go all around the world,
we can go to England and then…
we can sing, we can play
buzz disk everyday.
Let's make music again!

Verse 9 Let's go all around the world,
we can go to Germany and then…
we can sing, we can play
jingle bells everyday.
Let's make music again!

Verse 10 Let's go all around the world,
go to Nigeria and then…
we can sing, we can play
shekere everyday.
Let's make music again!

Verse 11 Let's go all around the world,
to the Sioux nation and then…
we can sing, we can play
frame drum everyday.
Let's make music again!

Verse 12 Let's go all around the world,
all around the world and then…
we can sing, we can play,
we can dance the day away.
Let's make music again!

Reproducible Lyric Sheet